On and Off the Fairway

A PICTORIAL AUTOBIOGRAPHY

BY *Jack Nicklaus* WITH *Ken Bowden*

SIMON AND SCHUSTER · NEW YORK

Published by Simon & Schuster
A Division of Gulf & Western Corporation
Simon & Schuster Building
Rockefeller Center
1230 Avenue of the Americas
New York, New York 10020

Designed by Irving Perkins
Manufactured in the United States of America
Printed by The Murray Printing Company
Bound by The Book Press, Inc.
1   2   3   4   5   6   7   8   9   10

Library of Congress Cataloging in Publication Data

Nicklaus, Jack.
    On and off the fairway.

    1.   Nicklaus, Jack.   2.   Golfers—United States—
Biography.   I.   Bowden, Ken.   II.   Title.
GV964.N5A34   796.352′092′4 [B]   78-15160

ISBN 0-671-22568-5

To the many thousands of people
all over the world, known and unknown,
who helped make it all possible,
but most of all to my mother

Appreciations

Of the many people who contributed to the making of this book, I would like to offer my deepest thanks to the photographers of golf around the world, many of them friends, not only for their contributions to these pages, but for their understanding and tolerance on and around the game's playing fields. Theirs is a tough job and, with almost no exceptions, they do it with grace, goodwill and good cheer.

I must also once again thank my literary collaborator, Ken Bowden, a good friend as well as a good writer, as much for his patience and insight as for his commitment and hard work. My appreciation, too, to another friend, Ken's wife, Jean Bowden, for her research and organizational contributions.

Finally, my thanks to Peter Schwed, a fine tennis player but an even better editor, for his aid, expertise and encouragement with this and all my previous authorship efforts.

Contents

Picture Credits

Some Introductory Reflections

I've always felt that I've had a lot of good luck in my life. Putting this book together has reinforced that feeling. Everybody is bound to have some bad times, and the pictures and recollections that follow include some of mine. But they are surprisingly few compared with the happy times recalled herein.

I suppose the most fortunate thing ever to happen to me was to be able to earn a living playing a game. I'd have to believe that most people in the world do what they do for a livelihood much more out of necessity than desire. I've never had to do that. Golf to me is not a vocation—it's an *avocation*. I began to play the game because I liked it, and I've gone on playing it simply because I love it. I may not sound very convincing to some people when I say that the money and applause have always been incidental, but that's the truth. Neither have ever motivated me to try harder or play better. What has is just the sheer challenge of the game itself, of doing something as well as I possibly can purely for the enjoyment of that effort and the personal satisfaction I enjoy when I'm

successful. I happen to believe that most high achievers have the same motivation. I also happen to believe that when they lose it, or begin to put the rewards ahead of the fun of doing one's best for its own sake, is when they begin to fail.

I've been fortunate, too, that golf has never become a mania. I admired my dad more than any other man I've known, and as the years have passed I've come to realize that the most admirable thing about him was his balance, his all-aroundness. My father was open to and interested in just about everything that life offered; he enjoyed the *adventure* of living to the fullest of his capacity. Very early on, I recognized the same qualities in Bobby Jones, which made me admire him just as much as I admired his legendary golfing achievements.

The result is that I have been able to develop a life of diversity in which many things are important but none so important that it consumes me. Looking around, especially on the pro tour, I believe this to be a healthy approach to living and one that I am very lucky to possess. Above all, it means that I can accept failure as well as I can success. People often seem surprised that I don't exhibit some sort of emotional trauma or go into a psychological decline following close defeats such as those I experienced in the 1977 Masters, British Open and PGA Championship. I want to win at everything I do, and I try to give everything I do my absolute best effort. But if, having done that, I lose, then so be it. Life goes on. This is especially true of a *game*, which to me is all that golf really is. After all, there will be many more days for golf, and there are a million other interesting things to do in this wide and fascinating world in between them.

As I think this book reflects, the most important thing in my life by a long way is my family. I am never satisfied that I have actually done my best for and with Barbara and our children, but I am sure they know that they have always come first in my scheme of things and always will. I have become more and more conscious of this as the children have grown older. There is not an awful lot a father can do with his kids when they are toddlers, which makes it very easy, at a time when you are building a career, to get out of the habit of doing things with them. Then, all of a sudden, they are growing up and beginning to go off in their own directions, and you find you've never really enjoyed them, never really gotten to know them. When you have five, as we do, and each begins to develop different interests, a lot of time is necessary to cover all the bases. I've always tried hard to find that time,

and I'm going to be trying harder still over the next ten to fifteen years, whatever the cost might be in terms of my golf career or business opportunities. In fact, it was this determination to meet what I see as my responsibilities as a father, and to enjoy my family to the full, that largely motivated the reduction in my playing schedule at the end of 1977.

The second-most-important thing in my life remains the game of golf. Because it has always been for me essentially a game, and because it is only one of many activities I enjoy, I have never become more than passingly tired of playing golf.

Naturally, my attitudes and goals have changed over the years. My first burning desire—and it seems a long way away now—was, of course, to learn to play golf as well as I could in the technical shot-making sense. Next came the desire to learn how to compete at the game successfully, which is a totally different kettle of fish from learning to play the shots. Then came the desire to work myself toward the top. Having got there or thereabouts, naturally I wanted to stay there a while. Having set a few records in fulfilling that goal, I would like to extend those records as far as possible, not only for my own satisfaction, but also to provide an exciting target for other golfers, present and future. Certainly, Bobby Jones's record of thirteen major championships was a tremendous stimulus to me. I like to think that whatever record I might be able to establish would be a similar stimulus both to other golfers and to the game generally.

10

No matter how greatly a player may be motivated by money at the outset of a career, inevitably there comes a point where, if it doesn't exactly become meaningless, money in and of itself is no longer a sufficient spur to attain and sustain maximum performance. That's the point where making or breaking records becomes the goal. I would feel I had contributed something worthwhile to the game of golf if it was my record that helped to heighten future aspirations and improve future playing standards. Incidentally, I have no doubt at all that whatever records I or anyone else may set, they will be broken someday, because that's simply the nature of competition—and a wonderful thing about sports.

Obviously, the maximum number of major championship wins remains my chief goal. What do I think that maximum might be? Well, the future is always unpredictable, but given the sort of health I currently enjoy, I see no reason why my best years aren't still ahead of me.

To permit publication of this book in 1978, I had to stop writing at the end of 1977. But I did get off to quite a good start in 1978, with two wins and two seconds in my first five tournaments, and then just in time to squeeze it into the book before it went to press, in July, I won the British Open for the third time. (See note, top of page 54.)

I'm probably more physically fit now than at any time since I left college, and I intend to keep myself that way. I'm not as long a hitter as I used to be, but I'm long enough—and I'm one heck of a lot better

shotmaker with every club in the bag than I've ever been. I've matured a lot mentally and emotionally in the past five years, to the point of seeing no great problems ahead on those fronts. The key factor, then, is the matter of desire. I am convinced that this is simply a question of pacing: of orchestrating my life in such a way as to keep myself "hungry" on the golf course.

That this had become a problem in 1977 was another reason for restructuring my playing schedule at the end of that year. Following the PGA Championship, I simply had no desire to play in the remaining tournaments to which I had allowed myself to become committed. Lacking the desire to play, I also lacked the will to *prepare* myself properly for those events, and it was this that really started me thinking hard about the future. If there has been one "secret" to whatever success I have had at golf, it has been preparedness, both physical and mental. In fact, I feel that this is what has separated me most from other tour players, so many of whom either don't appear to know how to prepare themselves or are so busy not missing a weekly paycheck that they never have the time or energy to get themselves totally ready for a 100 percent effort.

Knowing that I was improperly prepared had the effect of undermining both my confidence and my concentration, which led to sloppy performance. This in turn made me feel that I was doing not only myself and my reputation an injustice, but also the sponsors who'd used my participation to sell tickets and the fans who'd bought them on the assumption that I would be giving my best. In short, I angered and embarrassed myself to the point of deciding never again to let myself get into such a frame of mind. So, although I still can't say exactly what my playing schedule will be in the years immediately ahead, I can definitely say, first, that it will be less extensive than in the past twenty years and, second, that it will be geared primarily to preparing properly for the tournaments that I most want to win. That way, I feel pretty confident about remaining "hungry" for quite a time to come. Of course, should Tom Watson or Johnny Miller or Ben Crenshaw or anyone else really start piling up major titles, inevitably that hunger will become even keener.

The third-most-important consideration in my life today is my business activity. It is in the nature of most athletes to want to capitalize on their achievements, primarily to build long-term security during an inevitably short playing career, but also because the proceeds of so doing are a tangible and sometimes lasting measure of the success of their efforts. I've always had a third motivation, which is the sheer enjoyment of exercising and stretching my mind in a field completely removed from golf. It was this motivation, plus the desire to manage my own destiny, much more than any serious dissatisfaction with Mark McCormack, which caused me to separate from him in 1970 and to put together my own team of business associates under my own direct control.

I have rarely talked publicly about my business life, but this does seem an appropriate place to discuss at least the general policies that I feel underlie our business activities, particularly as these may differ somewhat from the usual attitudes of athletes and/or their business advisers.

The first concerns credibility. No matter how profitable the opportunity or how great my financial needs at the time, I have always disliked the thought of associating myself with products or services that I couldn't believe in and use with pride and enthusiasm. The result has been a lot of "No thank you's" to a great deal of money over the years, but also a clear conscience about everything I have involved myself with. This policy has also paid great dividends over the long haul in terms of the quality of both the products and services I speak for and the people behind them. As many top golfers and other sportsmen have painfully discovered, it becomes very difficult to enter the high end of the market once you've identified yourself with the low end. The high end, although perhaps less profitable at the beginning, will provide more stability and growth over the long haul.

Tenure is another important factor in our approach to all business enterprises. Maybe some get-rich-quick deals do work, but they never have for me because I've never let one past the door. We insist upon a minimum of five years for any association, because only in that way, we believe, is it possible to obtain total commitment from both sides. Ideally, we prefer a minimum of ten years, and most of my more

12

successful enterprises have at least that tenure.

Commitment has always been a big word in my approach to golf, and it is equally big in my business philosophy. I have, for example, made it an inflexible rule never to enter into an association in which I cannot make a full personal commitment of ideas, expertise, interest and time. That is why we are proud to call our involvements in the commercial world "partnerships" rather than endorsement arrangements.

The final but the most important consideration in any business involvement I undertake—or any other relationship, for that matter—is fairness. If an arrangement will not work equally well for all parties, in both human and financial terms, then I am not interested in pursuing it. This may not be a way to make a lot of money fast, but we have found it to be an excellent way to develop strength and stability in the marketplace—and, not incidentally or unimportantly, also a super way to make and keep friends.

One final thought on business. Just about every time I've lost a tournament in recent years, one or more writers have decided that the reason is my involvement in business, which, they usually go on to suggest, wears me out mentally or keeps me from the practice tee or weakens my concentration or builds boardroom jerks into my putting stroke or whatever. Sometimes I've been tempted to use this as an excuse myself, but I find it difficult not to be honest, and the truth is that it just isn't the case. The truth is that if I didn't have something to exercise and stretch my mind beyond hitting a golf ball, I'd go nuts.

Like everyone else, I sometimes overdo things: business, family concerns, recreation—even, as in the latter part of 1977, golf. But among my blessings is the ability not only to quickly identify such imbalances but to rapidly discipline and organize myself back to what for me is a normal and well-rounded if full and energetic life. So whatever the area of overindulgence, it is always brief and thus never permanently hurtful. Within this scheme of things, business, by taking me more completely away from golf than any other activity, is actually what most keeps me hungry to get back to it. And, as I mentioned a little while ago, there's nothing like hunger to keep a man going forward.

Seven Ages of Man

I wanted to get this in early to get it over with!

I was three months old in the first picture and five years old in the second.

The third picture was taken at the 1956 Ohio State Open, which I won with final rounds of 64-72. I was sixteen, and it was my first win outside of local Columbus or state junior competition. I weighed 175 pounds, which was the lightest I'd be until I hit the same weight again in the winter of 1976.

The fourth picture was taken three years (and twenty pounds) later, during college. The haircut was your basic jock style in those days.

I'd just won the 1963 Masters in the next picture. That's my first green jacket I'm wearing—along with the wet-look hairdo. This was around my heaviest time: I'd gone to around 210 to 215 pounds soon after I got married in 1960, and what with Barbara's wonderful cooking, it was very easy to stay there. However, I guess the real reason I did stay there was that I wasn't concerned about looks in those days—I was concerned about how I

played golf. Being heavy gave me strength. In fact, I was probably stronger, and hit longer, around this time than at any other point in my life—certainly much stronger than I am now, even if you take the age difference into account. Another factor was that my doctor, although he suggested I might one day have to lose weight if I began to tire easily, told me to stay the way I was, at least for the time being. With the changes in medical knowledge and attitudes, a doctor today probably wouldn't do that, but in those days you'd have been more likely to hear a trainer advise weight reduction than a regular GP, particularly if a fellow was as solidly fleshed and heavily muscled and physically active as I was. Anyway, the weight didn't worry me for a long time. Nor did the fact that most people my age had started wearing their hair longer and dryer. In fact, I was so busy with golf, I don't think I even noticed my appearance until about five years after this picture was taken.

I started losing weight toward the end of 1969, which was when the sixth picture was taken. What motivated me was getting tired for the first time in my life playing thirty-six holes a day in the Ryder Cup matches at Royal Birkdale in England. So when I returned home, I immediately went on a Weight Watchers-type diet and here was down to about 190 pounds. Then I went out and finished first, first and second in three consecutive tournaments—Kaiser, Sahara and Hawaii—and decided to spend even less time at the table.

In the last picture, taken in 1975, I was about 180 pounds, and since then I've regarded that as my median. These days I fluctuate between 175 and 185 pounds, depending on the time of year and how much exercise I'm getting. I still love to eat, but I keep it under control: one day steaks and macaroni and ice cream, then tuna fish and broccoli for the next two or three.

And the hair? Well, that just came with the rest of it. Being slimmer made me more clothes-conscious, and my sons were getting into the longer hairstyles. I got to where I am in the last picture in slow stages, and that's about as much hair as I've ever had. Recently, I've been keeping pace with the trend toward slightly shorter styles, but I don't think I'm ever going to go back to picture four—at least, not unless my hair starts to fall out.

And I'm not going back to 210 pounds, either, although I'm sure I'd hit the ball farther if I did.

Chapter 1
Getting Started

Getting Started

1950   age 10

Started golf and shot 51 for first nine holes
ever played

1953   age 13

Ohio State Junior Champion (13-to-15-year-
olds)
Columbus Junior Match-Play Champion
Won three matches in first national
championship, the USGA Juniors
Lost in quarterfinals of Columbus District
Amateur

1954   age 14

Scioto Junior Club Champion, holing in one
for first time in final round
Columbus Junior Match-Play Champion
Columbus Junior Stroke-Play Champion
Medalist in Tri-State (Ohio, Indiana,
Kentucky) High School Championship
Lost in second round of USGA Juniors
Finalist in Columbus District Amateur
Lost in first round of Ohio State Amateur
(won by Arnold Palmer)
Played on Upper Arlington High School team

1955   age 15

Columbus Junior Match-Play Champion
Columbus Junior Stroke-Play Champion

Ohio Jaycees winner
Tied for medalist in National Jaycees
Lost in quarterfinals of USGA Juniors
Columbus District Amateur Champion
Medalist in Ohio State Amateur
Qualified for U.S. Amateur for first time,
losing in first round

1956   age 16

Ohio State Junior Champion
Medalist in Tri-State High School
Championship
Ohio Jaycees winner
Lost play-off in National Jaycees
Lost in semifinals of USGA Juniors
Lost in quarterfinals of Ohio State Amateur
Ohio State Open Champion
Fifth in Sunnehanna Amateur Invitational
Lost in third round of U.S. Amateur

1957   age 17

Central Ohio High School District Champion
Ohio High Schools State Champion
Ohio Jaycees winner
National Jaycees winner
Lost in third round of USGA Juniors
Qualified for U.S. Open for first time, missing
cut by ten shots with 160
Lost in fourth round of U.S. Amateur

Early Form

These pictures were taken on the tenth tee at the Scioto Country Club in July 1953, when I was thirteen and really beginning to get into golf. I'd been playing for three years, and my handicap at this point was plus three. I remember that because an eighth-grade teacher, Mrs. Helen Tanner, was very surprised when she learned about it. I walked into class one day and she said, "Why, Jack, I just looked in the paper this morning and they printed all the district handicaps and you're the lowest!"

Unfortunately, these pictures don't truly reflect my swing at that time because they were posed. But some things haven't changed. For example, my right thumb still comes off the club today as it did then,

as you can see in the top-of-the-backswing picture. The cocking of the chin to make way for a full shoulder turn without swaying the head was there then too. It's obvious that my grip is pretty strong here, because the clubface is in a fairly closed position at the top, which explains why I hooked the ball a lot in those days.

Actually, these pictures were taken on a very significant day in my life. Two days previously, I'd played in a best-ball tournament in Lancaster, Ohio, and shot an 88 (despite that, we won the tournament because my partner shot a 65). The next day, I played in a celebrity event with Patty Berg in Columbus, shanked every iron shot I hit, and scored 53, which was two shots higher than my very first nine-hole score—and a very humiliating experience. I'd been feeling pretty sick for most of the

19

previous two weeks, and the way the pants look here shows how much weight I'd lost in that time—about twenty pounds. But the worst problems were backache and a persistent dull headache.

Anyway, I continued to play golf. During the afternoon, after these pictures had been taken, my dad came out and got me off the second hole at Scioto and told me I had to go to the doctor. My sister, Marilyn, had just learned that she had contracted polio. After the doctor examined me, he told me that I'd had it too—in fact, was just then recovering from it. I was very lucky, but my sister less so. The disease affected one of her legs, and she couldn't walk properly for quite a time. Fortunately, she recovered about 95 percent over the next few years.

Early Scoring

I'm often asked how fast I actually progressed at golf back in those early days. My clearest memory is that it was never as fast as I wanted, but here for the record are the numbers.

I was ten the first time I played nine holes—about three months after my dad got me started in the game and shortly after I'd begun taking lessons from Jack Grout—and I shot a 51. I immediately went backward, never breaking 60 for weeks thereafter. (But I already had the chat down pat. When anyone asked how I was playing, I'd say, "I'm hitting the ball great, but I just *can't score!*") I was, how-

ever, practicing and playing every day and by the end of the summer had managed a 91 for eighteen holes. The following year, aged eleven, I got down to 81, in the qualifying round for the Columbus District Junior Championship (losing in the first round to Larry Snyder, an elderly fellow of thirteen).

Naturally, by then the only thing on my mind was getting into the 70s, and after shooting three straight 80s, I finally achieved that in the summer of 1952, aged twelve, with a 74. Now, of course, paradise loomed: a round under 70. After months of almost unbearable frustration, I finally entered it early the following summer, with a 69, playing at Scioto with my father late one evening. We had intended only nine holes, and after congratulating me on an outward 34, Dad insisted we go home for dinner. Fortunately, I prevailed with my pleas for us to go out again after we ate, and I just made the magic number by eagling the par-5 eighteenth hole with a thirty-five-foot putt in almost total darkness.

Until then, all my golf had been local, but I think it was the commitment to the game that this level of scoring indicated, as much as the scores themselves, that persuaded my father to let me test my wings in faster company. At any rate, two weeks after the polio scare, and fully fit again, I made my first long-distance golfing trip, to Tulsa, Oklahoma, for the USGA National Junior Championship at Southern Hills, the first of many happy travels with my father. This picture was taken after my first-round win over Stan Zie-

My score that time out was 64, and I was regularly putting together some pretty good ones for my age—fourteen. This 64 on a par-68 course, with a 29 on the back, was a personal best at the time, but I followed it with five 63s in 1955, all of them admittedly on the comparatively short (6,400 yards) Ohio State Gray Course.

Strangely enough, I then went ten years without equaling that score, until the 1965 Australian Open at the Kooyonga course in Adelaide. And even then, it didn't mean much, because Gary Player shot one of the great scores of all time—264 for the seventy-two holes, including a pair of 62s.

browski. At thirteen and a half, I was the youngest qualifier from a then record field of 714 entered from forty-one states and Canada, and I was pleased to get through three rounds. The winner was a seventeen-year-old, Rex Baxter, who later became a tour player.

Five 63s

Here's the first trophy I won against competition from outside my home state—for medalist in the 1954 Tri-State High School Championship (Ohio, Indiana and Kentucky).

Dad

Here, I'm getting a pointer from Dad prior to a local tournament in 1955. My father rarely offered me advice without an invitation, but when I did ask for his thoughts, I listened to them carefully because he was extremely knowledgeable about all aspects of the game. Although he'd given up golf on graduating from Ohio State in 1935, prior to that he had been a good enough player to set a couple of course records around town. He never got back to that form after taking up the game again in 1950 as therapy for an ankle injury, but the exposure to top-level golf he enjoyed through his interest in my activities continually deepened his already acute insights.

Beyond the fact that he launched and supported me in the game for so many years, and his constant companionship, my father's great gifts to me were his selflessness and the rocklike solidity of his character. I've never known anyone with a sounder set of values and a better sense of perspective on all facets of life than Charlie Nicklaus, and I've never had a better friend.

Stroke-Building

Sixteen, and just not enough time in the day for golf! I practiced everything an awful lot in those days—I'd often putt well into the evening if there was enough moonlight to see the ball.

The basics don't seem to have changed much over the years. Setup is still very much the same, and the eyes-over-the-ball posture. One definite change is my left-hand grip. Here, it's pretty much on top of the club, but in later years I moved it considerably more to the left. My right hand is a bit farther behind the club now too, in more of a pistonlike "pushing" position, which helps me to keep the clubface square and on line.

Widening Horizons

Two happy guys at the National Jaycees Juniors in 1955. I was fifteen, and this was the first time I made any sort of mark nationally. I thought I'd won the medal, but Dick Foot came in and tied me at 144 and then beat me in a play-off. The fellow with me is Frank Eldridge, who was third.

Two Highlights

This was the golfing highlight of my high school days—and maybe the first time it ever vaguely occurred to me that the game might one day offer career possibilities. I'd just won the Ohio State Open at the Marietta Country Club with rounds of 76-70-64-72. The fellow with me is Earl Christiansen, who was second and low pro, three shots back. There were a number of good professionals in the field, including Frank Stranahan, and as you can tell from my face, I was one happy sixteen-year-old.

There's quite a story behind that third-round 64. Some time before this tournament, I'd been invited to play an exhibition with Sam Snead at the Urbana Country Club, in another part of Ohio, on the Friday afternoon of the Open. It was a treat I definitely didn't want to miss, so Bob Kepler, who was running the event (and who later became my good friend and golf coach at OSU), kindly fixed me an early starting time. Warren Grimes, who was putting the exhibition together and who was in the aviation business, then arranged to have me flown up to Urbana and back that day in a private Beechcraft D-18. That's how I got to meet and play with Sam for the first time.

Apart from the fact that he kept calling me "Junior" (Sam apparently calls anyone under thirty-five "Junior"), it was a marvelous experience. Generally, I kept up with the great man from the tee, but when it came to iron play, I quickly realized I still had a great deal to learn about golf. What really impressed me most, however, was Sam's superb rhythm and tempo. Naturally, I tried to imitate it, and my 64 the next morning owed a great deal to his example. So, since then, have a lot of other good scores I've compiled following rounds with Sam in practice or as a playing partner on the tour.

The picture page 24, left, was also taken during the 1956 Ohio State Open. I can't remember where the ball went, but on the evidence of the finish, this must have been a good strong swing. Notice the sole-plate of the MacGregor driver I'm using: the shape indicates that it was late-1940s vintage, which is the same model of driver I still use today. I have, incidentally, played MacGregor ever since I got my first full set of new clubs (Tommy Armours) at age eleven.

Baldie

No, Baldie wasn't a prize, although I'd have been glad to take him home with me—I've always loved dogs. He was an old English sheepdog who seemed to be around the Ohio State University golf courses almost as much as I was. He belonged to Bob Kepler, the OSU golf coach and a very good friend to me and a lot of other golfers in our early years.

I was seventeen here and had just won the Central Ohio High School District Championship. The good form held long enough for me to also win the Ohio High Schools State Championship the following week.

Another Favorite Game

I know I'd never have been able to make a career of basketball, but I love the game dearly. I think basketball is a marvelous sport—certainly the team sport I best like to play. I've played it on and off all my life and more and more in recent years since helping to build a fine gymnasium at my children's school in Florida. I'm a regular player there two or three times a week and a spectator at the school games whenever I'm home.

The picture here is of the Upper Arlington High School team in my senior year, and a pretty good team it was, too, at 16 and 4 for the season. I'd played football and baseball and run track in junior high, but by this time I'd pretty much given them up for golf and basketball. And if you'd asked me on this particular day what was my favorite sport, I'd probably have told you basketball.

I'm number 11, in case you missed the big smile (and thighs!). The fellow wearing number 14 is my cousin, Jim Nicklaus, who later became a fine baseball player, a very talented catcher. Even today I sometimes am given credit for his catching, which is flattering but incorrect and unfair to Jim.

First National Title

This was another very big day for me: the U.S. Jaycees Junior Championship in 1957, my first national title. I'd tied for medalist on my first try in 1955 and lost in a play-off in 1956 to Jack Rule. I got home here in my third and last attempt by, I think, two shots over John Konsek, a regular and very tough rival around that period who is now an eminent internist in Wisconsin. This tournament has helped a lot of youngsters over the years, and it was very good to me—I received a $1,000 scholarship that helped a lot with college expenses and also allowed me to go to the school of my choice, Ohio State, where I'd wanted to go since I was about six years old.

Making the presentation here is a gentleman who in later years became a good friend, John Brown. Coca-Cola sponsored the tournament, and John worked for the company. The blond girl at the far left of the picture is Mary Ward, whom I was dating at the time, and that's my sister, Marilyn, next to her. A cousin, Pete Nitschke, is over my left shoulder—golf was definitely a family affair even in those days!

High School Graduation

I didn't wear ties much at that time, but this occasion obviously called for it.

I suppose I wasn't too bad a student in those days, but there's no doubt what came first: sports and girls, in that order. Like so many fellows looking back from the perspective of mid-life, I'd probably have tried harder academically if I'd known then what I know now.

Chapter 2
Getting Serious

Getting Serious

1958   age 18

Trans-Mississippi Champion
Shot 67-66-76-68 for twelfth place in first pro
    tour tournament, the Rubber City Open
Finished in U.S. Open for first time, in forty-
    first place
Lost in second round of U.S. Amateur to
    Harvie Ward, one down

1959   age 19

North-South Amateur Champion
Played in first Masters, missing cut by one
    shot with 150
Played in first Walker Cup Match, winning
    foursomes and singles matches
Won Royal St. George's Challenge Vase ·
    (England)
Lost in quarterfinals of British Amateur
Trans-Mississippi Champion
Qualified for U.S. Open, missing cut with 154
U.S. Amateur Champion

1960   age 20

International Four-Ball winner (with Deane
    Beman)
Tied for low amateur and thirteenth place
    overall in Masters

Runner-up in Big Ten Championship
Runner-up to Arnold Palmer in U.S. Open by
    two strokes after leading with six holes to
    play
Lost in second round of NCAA Championship
Won both singles and both foursomes
    matches in first Americas Cup appearance
Lost in fourth round of U.S. Amateur
Medalist in World Amateur Team
    Championship with 66-67-68-68—269 at
    Merion, leading U.S. team victory

1961   age 21

Western Amateur Champion
Low amateur and tied for seventh in Masters
Tied for thirty-eighth in Colonial National
    Invitational (PGA event)
Tied for fourth in U.S. Open
NCAA Champion
Tied for twenty-third in Buick Open (PGA
    event)
Tied for fifty-fifth in American Golf Classic
    (PGA event)
Won Walker Cup foursomes and singles
    matches
U.S. Amateur Champion for second time
Won both foursomes and halved both singles
    in Americas Cup matches
Turned professional November 8

College

Things have changed a lot now, perhaps for the better, but in my day it was vital to join a fraternity if you wanted any kind of social life during college; and it certainly didn't do you any harm to be an athlete, either. I joined Phi Gamma Delta and lived in the fraternity house during my sophomore and junior years. Here's our freshman pledge class: a pretty small group, but it got bigger as the year went on, and we ended up with a really super bunch of guys. Many are still pals. (Obviously we all went to the same haberdasher for those ties!)

As in high school, I probably gave a little too much time to sports and not quite enough to classes at Ohio State, especially in my later years there. It surely was an energetic life. I played intramural basket-ball and football, fast-pitch softball, intra-fraternal volleyball and a little tennis; I water-skied in summer, and I fished whenever I could after Bob Kepler first got me interested by taking me up to the Zanesfield Rod and Gun Club (where I'm still a member). When I wasn't doing any of those things, or trying to keep up with a slim, blond and very popular young lady named Barbara Bash, I was usually play-ing handball at the athletic club. And then, of course, there was golf, lots of golf—which was really what finally pre-vented me from graduating.

Looking back, I guess the big mistake I made was taking pre-pharmacy for the first three years, because, having completed that with pretty good grades, I turned it into a waste of time by deciding that phar-macy wasn't the way I would want to earn my living. So in my senior year I transferred to the College of Commerce, majoring in insurance. This seemed more compatible with my growing aspirations as an amateur golfer, especially after Barbara Bash and I got married and I could begin to earn us some sort of living by actually selling insurance while studying it.

But the golf just grew too fast. I was simply away from school too often and for too long, and although I went back in the fall after my first year on the tour, the dean of the Commerce College came to me and told me to drop out. The reason was that he did not want a registered student of OSU being publicized as playing golf all over the world. It was a position I fought bitterly and still resent to this day. However, I badly wanted my degree after five years on and off at the university, and being within very close reach of the necessary hours, so for a while I took correspondence courses from the University of Wisconsin. Finally I realized that I'd already made up my mind a year previously about how I was going to earn a living, so I said to heck with it and decided to stick to golf. Obviously that hasn't been too painful a road to follow. But I am often sorry about not finishing school, because it's the one big thing in my life that I started and didn't complete.

Barbara

Barbara and I met the first week we were in college, when we were both seventeen. We seemed to do most of our

courting at sports events, but occasionally we'd find a more orthodox setting. Here, we were eighteen, at her parent's home.

Below, we were all set for a "Gay Nineties" party (and a good one it was, too, because I'd just turned eighteen and could drink beer legally for the first time). Nobody has "Gay Nineties" parties anymore; they have "Gay Fifties" parties. My kids went to one just the other day, and it upset the heck out of me.

No. 1 Against the Big Boys

This was my first win in a national amateur tournament not restricted to juniors:
the 1958 Trans-Mississippi. It was played
at Prairie Dunes in Hutchinson, Kansas, a
fine and unusual golf course—perhaps the
closest conditions I've seen in the United
States to those of British links courses,
even though it's more than a thousand
miles from an ocean. The fellow with me
is Dick Norville, of Oklahoma City, whom
I beat 9 and 8 in the final. I always felt it
was this win that got me selected for the
1959 Walker Cup team, although the
USGA never lets on about such things.

These trophies, incidentally, are two of
the biggest I've ever won (although actually I only got to keep one). This summer was memorable for me, too, because
about a couple of weeks later I played in
my first PGA tournament, the Rubber City
Open, at Firestone, took the lead after two
rounds with 67-66 and then finished with
76-68 for twelfth place.

Jack Grout

When Jack Grout wrote a book a few
years ago, his publishers asked me for a
quote for the jacket. I told them there was
a lot I could say about him, but that the
essence of it was as follows: "Everything
I've achieved in golf, I've done with techniques taught to me by Jack Grout." Those
are the exact words they used, and I still
can't think of any better ones to sum up
what this fine man has meant to me, except to add that, as good a coach as he has
been, he has been an even better friend.

The picture here shows Jack and me in
1959 "working" on the blade putter I used
in winning both of my U.S. Amateur
championships (it had to be a posed shot
because neither of us ever did a thing to
that club!). He'd been teaching me then
for nine years, ever since he came to

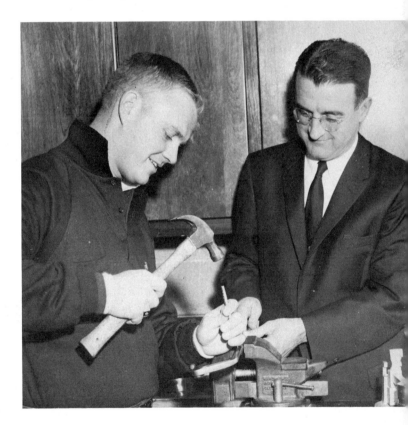

Scioto, which happened to be the year I started playing golf.

I still go to Jack for a complete refresher course in the fundamentals at the start of every season, plus periodic checkups and swing surgery when necessary. Now as then, his great talent is his simplicity: you never get any words from Grout until he's watched you long and carefully enough to figure out the *root* cause of whatever you are doing or not doing. Even then, you never get more words than are necessary to explain a particular fault and its cure. This is why he has always been and remains so fine a teacher of children and also of good players who already understand the basics of the game. Too many golfers are too full of technical trivia ever to be able to make a decent pass at the ball, and I think sometimes the fault lies in the sheer volume of needless information they pick up from overly detailed instruction.

At any rate, looking back, I'm sure that one of the greatest favors Grout did me was *not* to answer many of the hundreds of nitpicky questions I bombarded him with about the whys and wherefores of the golf swing. With Jack, it was fundamentals or nothing, which is the only way to become a good player in the first place and to stay one for a decent length of time.

I Like It!

This picture—like a lot of the early ones—was taken by Bill Foley, at Scioto in the spring of 1959. Bill was the top newspaper sports photographer for many years in Columbus, and he remained a good friend until his death from cancer in June 1976.

I just wish I could do on every swing now what I was doing then. Basically my swing remains the same today, but with less weight and more years it simply isn't as powerful as the action you see here. I particularly like the "quietness" in the upper body and wrists as the legs and hips pull everything down, under and through. I'm staying "inside" the shot, a sure sign of which is the very stable right-foot position, with little if any heel lift at this point. If I had to pick just one picture to convey what I believe to be the source of power in golf, which is leverage, this would be very high on the list.

Off to Scotland

Winning the Trans-Miss in 1958 had set me thinking for the first time about the possibility of making the following year's Walker Cup team, which in turn got me thinking for the first time about my true capabilities as a golfer.

Up to that time, I certainly had aspirations about the game, but they weren't very clear-cut. Basically, at age eighteen, I just wanted to play as well as I could in as many tournaments as I could, while still getting an education and having a lot of fun at college. Suddenly it occurred to me that the Walker Cup squad represented

34

the nine or ten best amateurs in the country and that if I made the team I'd be one of those ten. It was a pretty scary thought, considering some of the players around in those days—Harvie Ward, Charlie Coe, Bill Hyndman, Billy Joe Patton, Bud Taylor, Bob Gardner, Gene Andrews, and a lot of others, most of them older and much more experienced than I was. My hopes of making the team weren't all that high because, apart from the Trans-Miss win and a first foray into the world of the pros just to see what it was like, I hadn't done an awful lot in 1958.

However, when the squad was announced, there I was on it, and I still get a kick now remembering the huge thrill it gave me. Obviously, the big excitement was representing my country, but the thought of going abroad for the first time—and especially to Scotland, the birthplace of golf—got me pretty tingly too.

Here I am with my mom, Helen Nicklaus, all spruced up and on my way. Actually, the bagpiper was only one part of the hoopla. My dad and all his friends, and seemingly all their friends, plus half the membership of Scioto—at least sixty or seventy people, as I recall—came out to Columbus Airport to see me off that happy day.

The Walker Cup

For me, and I think for a lot of other golfers who've been fortunate enough to participate in them, international team contests are the most enjoyable events in golf. If the game has one drawback, it is its individuality, its self-concernedness—its selfishness, to be blunt about the matter. Playing for a team, and particularly for your country in someone else's country, really brings a group of guys together.

That's pretty evident, I think, in this shot of seven of our 1959 Walker Cup squad during practice at magnificent Muirfield in Scotland, the home of

The Honourable Company of Edinburgh Golfers, one of the oldest golf clubs in the world. From left to right, after "Junior," are Billy Joe Patton, Deane Beman, Tommy Aaron, Ward Wettlaufer, Bud Taylor and Harvie Ward (Bill Hyndman and Charlie Coe were the other two team members).

This was, of course, the occasion when I first fell in love with the Muirfield course, to the point eventually, after my 1966 British Open win there, of naming my own course in Columbus after it. I also fell in love with the food and everything else at the marvelous little Greywalls Hotel that sits right behind the tenth tee.

37

My One British Amateur Attempt

Traditionally, the better American amateurs have played in the British Amateur only when they would be making the trip anyway for the Walker Cup, and that's how I got to take my one shot at this, the world's oldest amateur championship. It wasn't as successful as I would have liked—I lost in the quarterfinals to Bill Hyndman, my only loss at match play during the whole of 1959.

Here, I'm scraping through the fourth round against the Irishman Noel Foggarty at the first extra hole after a real humdinger of a match—my ball finished inches from the pin for a winning par 4. The course is Royal St. George's, the site of the last British Open to be played in southern England, in 1949. It's just about the ultimate in leave-it-as-the-Lord-made-it links courses, and it was fun apart from the large number of semi- and totally blind shots (I've never enjoyed hitting at things I can't see).

Deane

Deane Beman won that 1959 British Amateur and then went on to win the U.S. title the following year, a fine accomplishment.

He and I had been close friends and played a great deal of golf together for some years, but I think this—my repeat win in the Trans-Miss in 1959—was the first time we'd competed head-to-head in national competition. I got him by 3 and 2—and another of those huge trophies. Guess I won in the scalped look too!

The First Amateur

Here's my big moment of 1959, the U.S. Amateur at the Broadmoor Golf Club in Colorado.

I beat the defending champion and 1949 winner, Charlie Coe, one up over the thirty-six holes of the final in one of the toughest matches I've ever experienced. After a heck of a scrap all day long, and a dumb bogey by me on the thirty-fifth, we came to the last hole all square. In those days, it was a 430-yard par 4 doglegging right. We both hit excellent tee shots, then Charlie played an eight-iron that unluckily ran through the green and trickled down a bank into heavy grass. A few yards ahead of him off the tee, I put a nine-iron about eight feet short of the hole. Then,

39

with one of the finest recovery shots I've ever seen, Charlie played his ball within a half turn of going into the cup.

How I squeezed in that eight-footer I don't know, but somehow I did and about two days later woke up to the fact that I really was the U.S. Amateur Champion—and the second youngest in history, at that, to Bob Gardner, the 1910 winner. You can tell from the picture here how dazed I was. Presenting the trophy is John D. Ames, then president of the USGA and a good friend ever since.

Not Quite as It Looks

This is one of those pictures that newspapermen always like to take but that actually give a false impression, harmless as that may be in this case.

The scene here is the basement of our house in Columbus in the late fifties, and the spectators are, of course, my parents. What dedication, you might think, what desire! Well, here's the truth.

In planning the house, Dad thought it would be a great idea to set up a driving range in the basement. He built it ten and a half feet high instead of the usual seven or eight feet, and he also built it fifty-four feet long, so that we'd have room for a shuffleboard court as well as the driving net and a pool table. Well, in they all went, at great trouble and expense, and there they stayed—very rarely used after the novelty wore off in a couple of weeks.

One problem with the driving net was that a ball hit hard into the corners would ricochet off the cement-block walls and force everyone to take a very fast dive to avoid being decapitated. We did use the pool table quite a bit, but I can't remem-

ber anyone ever playing shuffleboard after the first few tryouts.

I guess the net did get periodic use from both my parents—certainly more than from me. Mom would occasionally beat away in it, but it never seemed to help her golf. I was raised by a very athletic father and a very enthusiastic mother, who has never let her lack of skill get in the way of her desire to play. She still plays golf quite often, and I believe her lowest score is *still* 119.

Incidentally, this picture makes it quite obvious who influenced my choice of hairstyle!

There's Always a Way

The last picture notwithstanding, I did practice a lot as a youngster, and that's one of the reasons for this intriguing contraption, once a feature of the driving range at Scioto. It's half a Quonset hut, with a gas heater that would, with luck and some coaxing, usually get the temperature inside up somewhere around 55 degrees. I seem to remember the initiative behind it being mainly my dad's, but quite a few of the keener fellows made use of the facility whenever there were any balls left to hit— which meant they had to get there before I did.

In those days, I'd quit golf almost totally around mid-October and then start hitting balls again from the hut—or outdoors if there wasn't too much snow or wind—early in January. I'd build up the sessions through February and early March and then take off for the South—usually Pinehurst, North Carolina, or Florida—during the spring college vacation, both for practice and for some warm-up tournament play. Then as now, the closer the Masters came, the harder I worked.

Once we were into the season proper, of course, I practiced and/or played almost daily. During the summer vacation, I virtually lived on the course—a few hundred practice balls and thirty-six holes was just a normal day's work. That's one reason I haven't had to hit millions of balls to stay in shape for the game in recent years—my basic swing was pretty much locked into a groove twenty years ago. Another reason is the very sound set of fundamentals I learned right at the outset from the man with the glasses watching me here, Jack Grout. As I've said, Jack started teaching me when I was ten, and he has been doing so ever since—beginning each year, as here in 1961, with a thorough review of the fundamentals.

Also along at this session is Bob Obetz, a good golfer and my best man a few months earlier.

Marriage

Wedding day, July 23, 1960, North Broadway Methodist Church, Columbus,

Ohio. I kidded Barbara that we picked that date because it was the weekend of the PGA Championship, for which, as an amateur, I was ineligible. In actuality, with the big step coming up, I'd thought little about golf since losing the U.S. Open to Arnold Palmer five or six weeks previously. However, I did make one grand golfing gesture before tying the knot. Playing the final hole at Scioto the day before, I suggested that everyone should step well back because, this being my final tee shot as a single man, I was really going to zing it. Muscles twanging, eyes popping, teeth grinding, I launched myself into the ball with all the power and fury I could muster—only to just tick the top of it and watch it, amid the hysteria of my friends, slowly trickle into a creek twenty yards from my nose.

Both the wedding and the wedding reception went a lot better than that effort—the reception a little too well in my case. Barbara had to drive us home for the only time in our lives, and if I hadn't had this piece of cake, she would probably have had to do it earlier. I've never been much of a drinker, and two or three can really get to me. Barbara didn't drink or smoke then and doesn't now. She might accept a vodka and tonic at the start of an evening out, but if you look at her at ten-thirty, usually half of it is still there. Actually, ten-thirty would usually be too late because she'd probably be home in bed. She's never been a swinger—in fact, it sometimes gets to my conscience how many darn things she does exactly right in life.

Much Commotion at Merion

In golf it was also a good year for me, with a tie for low amateur and thirteenth place in the Masters, second place to Arnold Palmer in the U.S. Open, and a 4-0 record in the first of the two Americas Cup matches I played for the United States.

But what really put the icing on this season was the World Amateur Team Championship at Merion at the end of September. Merion, in Ardmore, Pennsylvania, is rightfully regarded as one of the greatest courses in America, and in 1950 Ben Hogan had won the U.S. Open there in a play-off after shooting 72-69-72-74—287 for the regulation seventy-two holes. In World Amateur individual play, my score, which led the United States to the team championship, was 66-67-68-68—269. For a long time this caused a great deal of commotion around the world of golf, and once or twice in the middle of it, I was tempted to go along with what seemed to be the general consensus and say, "Yes, what a fantastic performance that was! All due to hard work and talent!" Mostly, however, I stuck with the truth, which is that there is no way to fairly compare my performance with Hogan's. When Ben won at Merion, the course had been fully prepared for a U.S. Open, which means narrow fairways, heavy rough and hard, fast greens. Also, I seem to remember being told that there was often a stiff wind during the 1950 Open.

When I won at Merion, the course was pretty much as the members play it in terms of fairway width and rough, there

was no wind whatsoever, and with lots of rain before and during the event, you could stop the ball on the green off a topped two-iron. (See the fashion-plate picture of me in the second round for an idea of how soggy everything was.)

In short, what Hogan did was to play superb golf under the prevailing conditions, and what I did was to play good golf under a totally different and much easier set of conditions.

Nevertheless, it was a marvelous end to the season for all the U.S. team members, as this picture indicates. From left to right, yours truly, Bill Hyndman, Bob Gardner, nonplaying captain Tot Heffelfinger, and Deane Beman.

Snowbirds

No, despite Barbara being along (and what a lot of fun she looks as though she's having!), this wasn't a "setup" picture.

This, along with the Quonset hut (see page 41), is how as an amateur I got ready for the season every year. When the snow wasn't too deep, I'd clear a patch of grass to hit from; when it was, I'd trample it down and hit balls right off the top of it. Usually I'd pick the balls up, but when the snow was too deep to find them, we'd leave them there until it thawed sufficiently. That's when everybody had to watch the balls in his shag bag: after hitting mine, I'd go through anyone else's I could find!

The year is 1961, incidentally.

45

The Three of Us

You can only see two? Well, the time is late March, 1961, and Barbara was three months pregnant with Jackie. She doesn't look that far along, but then she never has with any of the children.

The event, incidentally, was my first of that year, the Western Amateur, and obviously all that snow work paid off, because the win set me up for a very good year.

College Golf

Probably because my personal golfing horizons were expanding so fast, I didn't get to play golf for Ohio State until my junior year, 1960. I enjoyed it a lot from then on, and particularly our coach, Bob "Kep" Kepler, the man first responsible for me becoming a lifelong fishing nut.

I lost the individual title in the Big Ten Championship by two shots to John Konsek in 1960, and—a little down from finishing second in the U.S. Open the previous week—went out in the second round of the NCAA.

This picture was taken at the 1961 NCAA at Purdue University, which I got a big kick out of winning in my last year of eligibility.

I Like These Too!

Oh, boy! Was I ever strong in those days! Could I bust that ball! This was the summer of 1961, and some measure of how powerful I was around that time is that during the year I broke the face inserts out of nine drivers. That's never happened to me since, so either MacGregor has been making better golf clubs or I've been getting weaker!

Seriously, this was probably the strongest—and the longest—I've ever been: a good thirty pounds heavier than I am today and a good thirty yards longer on average with the driver. Obviously, you gradually lose strength as you get older, but there's no doubt that the weight reduction took something away too. I can still hit the ball almost as far as I did then when I absolutely have to, but I need a right-to-left flight instead of the fade I gave to everything in those days—and I usually also have to jump out of my socks to do it.

The consolation, of course, is that I'm

altogether a more complete golfer now than I was at that time. There's no way I could have played a controlled draw in those days, not to mention a whole arsenal of other shots. Basically, at twenty-one, I just hit the ball as far as possible off the tee, found it, hit it onto the green, then hit it into the hole. Rough wasn't any great problem, even though most of the tournaments I played were on lush, soft-grassed Midwestern- and Eastern-type courses, because I was usually close enough to the green and/or strong enough to just bulldoze the ball out of anything I found myself in, short of a young forest. Essentially,

I'd call this the "abandoned" approach to golf: hit it very hard, go after it, then hit it very hard again.

It was great fun and a very healthy approach to the game for a young amateur, but I quickly realized when I got on the pro tour the following year how much more thought and work lay ahead of me if I was ever to become the complete player I aspired to be. I've been thinking and working toward that goal ever since, of course, and still see no end to the learning process, which for me is one of the factors that makes golf such a fascinating game.

Apart from the raw power I'm putting

out here (probably trying to impress the photographer), the form itself looks pretty good. I've made a good backswing: a really strong turn-and-coil of the top half against the resistance of the lower half with no sway; hands high and firm; clubface in the same alignment as the back of the left hand; club shaft parallel to the target line; very nice foot and leg work. As I come down, the amount of torque I built going back is really doing its work, forcing the legs and hips to lead as a reflex action and pulling the hands and club back to the ball from well on the in-side of the target line—the one move most handicappers never seem to be able to master. Good foot action here too: weight solidly over to the left, with no premature right-heel lift to spin me "out and over." Coming into the hitting area looks equally solid: hips clearing as knees still drive; head well behind the ball; left arm pulling hard toward the target as the right hand begins hitting; shoulders squaring as the clubhead starts releasing.

In fact, it all looks so good I'm tempted to get a haircut and become a mountain again!

49

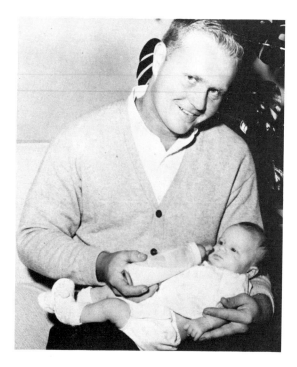

Jack II

Jack William II joined us on September 23, 1961, and obviously his arrival had a big bearing on a decision I was to make regarding my future a few weeks later.

Like most fathers, my feeding efforts diminished as the family grew and the older children helped out with the little ones. I think I fed Jackie a lot, Stevie fairly often, Nan occasionally, Gary once or twice, and Michael not at all.

The Second Amateur— and Beyond

Though the spot I'm in here (page 51) is one of the worst places to be in golf, the

picture brings back many happy memories. I'm behind the thirteenth green at Pebble Beach, and it's a spot I've tried very hard to avoid ever since, because the shot from there is virtually impossible no matter where they put the pin. The event was the 1961 U.S. Amateur, my second national championship and my last amateur win in an individual tournament. With me in the picture below is Dudley Wysong, who I'm glad to remember could still smile after losing in the final 8 and 6.

I played as well in this tournament as I have in any major championship and certainly better than in any other match-play event. The record book shows that I was twenty under par for the 112 holes of the eight matches I contested in; that I was under par in every match; that I lost only nineteen holes; and that I was never taken beyond the seventeenth hole except in the thirty-six hole semifinal and final (perhaps that's why I've always had trouble with

eighteen at Pebble Beach!). Even I will immodestly claim that that ain't bad on that particular golf course!

Actually, a couple of things bore on this performance beyond the fact that I just happened to be playing extremely well at the time. One was the inspiration I drew from Pebble Beach itself. It was my first visit to the course, and I fell in love with it immediately. It remains my favorite among all the six-hundred or so courses I have played around the world.

The second factor was that, for the first time in my life, instead of simply estimating distances, I knew exactly how far I had to hit the ball on every approach shot. This came about as a result of playing with old friend Deane Beman in practice. The course was strange and the winds blustery. I was having real problems judging distances, and I mentioned this to Deane. "Then why don't you pace them off?" said the ever astute Beman, who'd been doing just that himself for quite a time. It made sense. I started doing it right there and then, and I've been doing it ever since.

Not only that, but I've kept every annotated scorecard from every tournament course I've since played. As a matter of fact, I still have the first charted card from Pebble Beach (a copy of it, that is—the original's a mite worn), and I still use those 1961 marks and yardages in the Crosby every year. (The Crosby, incidentally, is the only tournament, other than the "big four," that I had never missed through 1978 since turning pro, which is about as strongly as I can emphasize my love for Pebble Beach.)

Following the 1961 Amateur, I played no serious competitive golf until the Americas Cup match at the Club Campestre Monterrey in Mexico in late October, my second trip outside the United States. By this point, it was becoming clear that some big decisions had to be made. I still greatly enjoyed the world and atmosphere of amateur golf, but actually competing was becoming less fun the more I was expected to win, which by then was every time I teed up. This would have been easier to live with if I had been able to devote myself entirely to golf. I wasn't in a position to do that, and it annoyed me not to be able to give the time and effort I felt I needed in order to fulfill both these outside expectations and my own ambitions.

Then, too, inevitably the prospect of graduating from college wasn't coming any closer with the amount of golf I was playing. Financially, I was comparatively well off for those days, earning about $24,000 a year from insurance sales and promotional work for a slacks company, but it was hardly secure income, especially in the light of our recent parenthood. Mostly, there was the nagging question of how to continue to develop and maximize my talents as a golfer and still be able to meet all my other responsibilities and work toward my other goals. To

be the best golfer I could become was definitely what I wanted most. But what I just couldn't settle my mind about was whether I could actually afford both the time and the cash to try.

It was a troubling period, and after talking a number of times with my dad, I decided to at least have a discussion with Mark McCormack about the obvious alternative: professionalism. Mark came to Columbus and was very helpful about the differences being a pro would make to our lives and what we might expect financially. In regard to the latter, he said that he felt I could almost certainly expect in my first year as a pro to earn not less than $100,000, beyond whatever I won on the golf course (as it happened, most of the things he talked to me about worked out as he projected). The prospect was tempting, but there were no immediate financial needs and, as the Americas Cup trip reaffirmed for me, I was still very much an amateur at heart.

Returning from that, I had virtually made up my mind to remain an amateur. In the next two weeks, I started looking ahead and began planning all the things I wanted to do with my golf game, and very quickly the sheer impracticality of my goals once again became sharply evident. I called a family council and also sought the advice of a number of good friends in amateur golf, and suddenly I made up my mind. On November 8, I announced I was turning professional.

As I've already said, it's a decision I've never regretted.

Chapter 3
The Majors

The Majors

1959–1977
Major championships entered: 71
Victories: 14
Second places: 14
Third places: 9
Top-three finishes: 37

FLASH!
In what I think may be the best major tournament I have ever played from tee to green, I won my third British Open on July 15, 1978 over the Old Course of the Royal and Ancient Golf Club at St. Andrews with a score of 281. This victory means that I am the only golfer in history ever to win all four of the major tournaments at least three times—no one else has ever won them all twice.

The Masters

*1959 Missed cut
*1960 Low amateur, tied 13th
*1961 Tied 7th
1962 Tied 15th
1963 Won
1964 Tied 2nd
1965 Won
1966 Won
1967 Missed cut
1968 Tied 5th
1969 Tied 24th
1970 Eighth
1971 Tied 2nd
1972 Won
1973 Tied 3rd
1974 Tied 4th
1975 Won
1976 Tied 3rd
1977 Second

The U.S. Open

*1957 Missed cut
*1958 Forty-first
*1959 Missed cut
*1960 Second

* Played while still amateur

*1961 Tied 4th
1962 Won
1963 Missed cut
1964 Tied 23rd
1965 Tied 31st
1966 Third
1967 Won
1968 Second
1969 Tied 25th
1970 Tied 49th
1971 Second
1972 Won
1973 Tied 4th
1974 Tied 10th
1975 Tied 7th
1976 Tied 11th
1977 Tied 10th

The British Open

1962 Tied 32nd
1963 Third
1964 Second
1965 Tied 12th
1966 Won
1967 Second
1968 Tied 2nd

1969 Tied 6th
1970 Won
1971 Tied 5th
1972 Second
1973 Fourth
1974 Third
1975 Tied 3rd
1976 Tied 2nd
1977 Second

The PGA Championship

1962 Tied 3rd
1963 Won
1964 Tied 2nd
1965 Tied 2nd
1966 Tied 22nd
1967 Tied 3rd
1968 Missed cut
1969 Tied 11th
1970 Tied 6th
1971 Won
1972 Tied 13th
1973 Won
1974 Second
1975 Won
1976 Tied 4th
1977 Third

Oakmont '62

I suppose, as such things go, I did not make too bad a start to my pro career. The opening effort wasn't anything to rave about—I tied for fiftieth in the Los Angeles Open with a 289 for $33.33—but by the time the U.S. Open came around I'd played in seventeen tournaments and placed second or third five times and in the top ten eight times.

The events that meant the most to me, then as now, were the majors, and for the same reasons: they have tenure and continuity, they are played on the best courses, they attract the finest fields, and as true championships run only for the benefit of the game, they are the tournaments that people enjoy watching the most and remember the longest.

I had disappointed myself by finishing worse (tied for fifteenth) in my first Masters as a pro than in my two prior efforts as an amateur (tied for thirteenth and seventh), and I was looking forward to the U.S. Open at Oakmont as a chance to redeem myself not only for that poor Augusta National effort, but also for the previous two U.S. Opens, in which, given excellent chances to win, I'd finished second and tied for fourth.

The picture here is of my opening drive at Oakmont, and it was a good long one right down the middle, for two reasons. First, a little more self-discipline at table and six months of almost continuous golf had gotten me into what I felt to be excellent physical shape at 202 pounds—probably not more than ten pounds over where

55

I should have been at that stage of life. Second, I had played very well at the Thunderbird Classic the previous week to finish runner-up to Gene Littler in the tour's first $100,000 tournament. So I felt exceptionally confident about my game.

As things worked out, the confidence was justified. Playing with Arnold Palmer the first two days, I shot 72-70 without really doing much with the putter, which reflects an excellent tee-to-green game on a "USGA-ed" course as big as Oakmont, then added a 72 and a 69 to tie Arnold. (There was a lot of talk that week about how well I putted and how poorly Arnold putted. The fact of the matter is that Arnold, although he three-putted something like thirteen times, single-putted about twenty-five greens; whereas, although three-putting just once, I single-putted only about eleven times. I'd call that roughly a draw.) In the play-off, I started with three birdies and then steadied down for a 71, which was good enough to win by three shots.

This obviously was the event that really set the Palmer-Nicklaus hullabaloo in motion, and I've often been asked since what I felt about Arnold in that championship. Well, Arnold was, of course, the absolute king at that time, not only as a golfer, but as one of the most charismatic and popular figures in world sports. Additionally, what with Oakmont being so close to his home, just about everybody in the gallery was at least a "general," and usually a four-star one, in his legendary "army." Maybe I was too emotionless at that time, or just plain dumb, but none of this really both-

ered me much. To me, in those earliest pro days, Arnold Palmer was just someone in my way, just another guy to beat on the road to where I wanted to go. It wasn't really until several years later that I started to think about what Arnie really had achieved in and come to mean to the game of golf. Perhaps some of that immaturity on my part, getting through to the fans as overconfidence or lack of proper regard for a living legend, was what made me such a black hat to so many of them in the years immediately ahead. But if I gave offense with anything but my golf clubs, it certainly wasn't through deliberate or conscious effort on my part.

Then as now, I respected Arnold greatly as a golfer and as a man, and I enjoyed playing with and against him. What I didn't see was why any of those feelings should stop me from trying to beat him on the golf course.

Here's my last hole of regulation play. I hit a super tee shot, dead down the middle

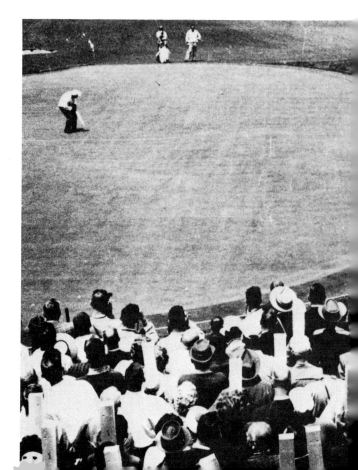

56

and very long, and I'll never forget the ovation I received as I walked off the tee: it was the kind that sends chills up and down your spine. I also hit a very good approach shot with a six-iron that unluckily rolled off the plateau where the pin was set. If this putt from about twenty feet had gone in, I would have won outright. Arnold actually had the same chance to win outright from much the same distance.

Here are Arnold and I after tying. You can't see them very well in this picture, but I was wearing what Barbara christened my "army refugee" pants. They were an iridescent olive that was really a bright pair of pants for me at that time— just a shade above neutral. I felt they'd brought me such good luck over the final thirty-six holes (which we played in one day at that time) that I wore them again in the play-off. They really were a wow— must have cost all of $8.95.

Bobby Jones got a New York ticker-tape parade on arriving back from his victories in the British Amateur and Open Championships in 1930. I got the same treatment in Columbus following the U.S. Open win. The cops estimated a turnout of ten to fifteen thousand, which means there were either an awful lot of people eating lunch in town that day or a whole lot more golfers in Columbus than I ever knew about. Seriously, it was a great gesture by my hometown people and typical of the marvelous support they have always given me.

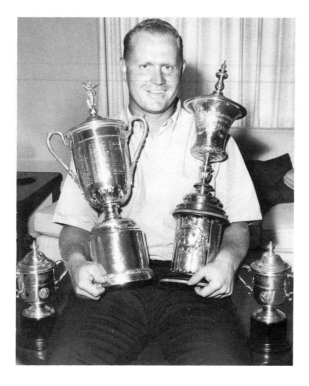

Winning at Oakmont made me only the third golfer to hold the Amateur and Open titles at the same time. The other two were Chick Evans, who won both titles in the same year, 1916; and Bobby Jones, who held them in 1925–26 and 1928–29, and then won both in 1930, his Grand Slam year. Here I am with the trophies.

Augusta '63

Here's a happy moment, my first Masters win. Although the scoring was high—my 286 tied the third-highest winning total up to that point—I played pretty good golf that week in rough weather to get in one ahead of Tony Lema.

Actually, the first memory this picture brings back isn't so much of the thrill of that moment, but of some out-of-character thinking it provoked. It's one of the very few false or contrived things I've ever come close to doing on a golf course—or anywhere else, for that matter. Walking up toward the green knowing that I needed only two putts to win the Masters, I suddenly started thinking and worrying about how I should react after I'd holed out. Perhaps people talking and writing so much about me seeming so cold and controlled was what prompted the thought. At any rate, after some deliberation walking up the fairway, I decided that I'd throw my hat and even got to thinking a little bit about the mechanics of how I'd throw it. But when I got to the green, I very nearly three-putted. Suddenly, when I made the second putt, there wasn't any need to figure out a particular way of reacting, because now I really *did* want to toss my hat in the air. Here it goes—and with real feeling.

To be more serious about this win, one aspect of it made a profound impression upon me that has borne very heavily on my career ever since. The worst weather of a generally untypical Masters week came in the third round. I was playing with Mike Souchak, who was leading after the first two rounds, and when we came to the thirteenth hole the entire fairway area on the hillside in the dogleg elbow seemed to be under water. Mike said to me, "You know, I don't think there's any way we're going to be able to finish today," and he just sort of slopped his way

through the rest of the hole and made a seven or eight. I felt Mike might prove to be right, but I decided to keep plodding on as best I could, not enjoying myself much, but not taking anything for granted, either.

Finally, when we got to eighteen, Mike was heading for a 79 and me for a 74, and for the first time I was close enough to a leader board to be able to distinguish between the red and the green numerals (I'm totally color blind with green at distances over forty or fifty yards and partially with red). There were a lot of *l's* on the board, designating the leaders' cumulative scoring in relation to par, but it looked to me as though there was only one such figure in red, meaning under par. I asked my caddie, Willie Peterson, whether this was correct. "Yes, sir! Only you, boss," said Willie, and suddenly I realized that

simply by hanging in there, I was leading in the Masters.

Later, when I reflected on that win, a deeper realization struck me that has since brought me a lot more first places, especially in the majors, where the added competitive pressures and the difficulty of courses can so easily frustrate and demoralize a golfer. This is that most golf tournaments are not so much "won" by opportunistic play as not lost when opportunity presents itself. It's a great realization for breeding patience and perseverance.

Good thing this picture was taken before dinner or I'd have had three or four more chins, I'm sure. I was the youngest-ever winner of the Masters, but I certainly didn't look it here! Even though Arnold, here presenting the green jacket as the previous year's

winner, was never really in contention in 1963, it was definitely one of my least popular wins. I'd been getting quite a bit of flack from fans on the tour, but I was very surprised to find myself so much the Black Knight at a place like the Augusta National, where the patrons were supposed to be so discerning about golf in addition to possessing all that Southern courtliness. Perhaps my worst moment that year came during the last round at Augusta. Sam Snead, always a big favorite there, was very much in contention and, playing immediately ahead of me, made a birdie at eleven. As it was going on the scoreboard, I bogeyed the hole, and a big cheer went up. Obviously, it hurt—a lot more than I hope I ever showed.

But, thankfully, that's all a long time ago, and things have taken a 180-degree turn. Funny how such basically superficial considerations as smiling and waving and changing the style of your hair and clothes can affect the public's impression of a fellow, isn't it?

Here's one of my favorite pictures, so much so that I've had one similar to it on the wall at home ever since. The gentlemen with me are Bob Jones (I'm giving him the ball I holed out with on the last green) and Cliff Roberts, the creators of both the Augusta National Golf Club and the Masters—and my very dear friends ever since my first invitation to Augusta in 1959.

Jones influenced my life more than any other man after my father, especially in terms of my overall attitude to golf and the structuring of my career. Roberts, when you got to know him, was a much warmer man than he appeared on the surface. But he was also the strongest-minded individual I've ever known: absolutely determined to have everything done the way he believed it should be done—which, incidentally, was usually the right way. Much as the manner of his death saddened me, it didn't surprise me, because if you knew Cliff you knew there was no way he could ever tolerate not being in control of his own destiny.

Dallas '63

Believe it or not, the hottest I've ever been at a golf tournament—off the course, at least—was at the 1976 British Open at Royal Birkdale. It was played right in the middle of an all-time-record British heatwave, and the old hotel we stayed in just wasn't built or equipped for such weather. Unable even to open many of the windows (they'd been nailed shut to prevent rattling in the more typical gales of the area), people slept with their bedroom doors wide open all night. Even then, it was like living in a sauna.

The hottest I've ever been physically *on* a golf course was here at the 1963 PGA Championship. And I was pretty hot mentally, too, just as this picture was taken, having left myself this tricky little four-footer for a bogey to win by one shot.

For a number of holes before this, I'd also had the British Open in mind, having bogeyed the last two holes to lose it the previous week at Royal Lytham and St. Anne's. Leading by two shots with one hole to play here at the Dallas Athletic Club, I hit a very poor tee shot into rough so deep that all I could do was chip out. I followed that with a good nine-iron to within twenty feet of the hole, but then darned if I didn't go and slide the thing by a good four feet, giving myself one of the most nervous moments I've ever had in a major. But the next ball went in, as the picture of Barbara and me with then PGA president Lou Strong indicates.

The interesting thing about this first PGA Championship win is that I went eight years before repeating—the longest

62

period to date [end of 1977] without a victory in one of the major championships since I began competing in them. That's a testimonial to the true caliber of a championship that's often unfairly regarded as being the weak sister among the four big ones.

In terms of its field, the PGA is actually the toughest of all to win, and it could easily become the toughest, period, if the courses used for it were consistently up to the standards of the U.S. Open (as they are fast becoming). As things stand, I rate the U.S. Open as both the toughest tournament in the world to win and the most important for any player who hopes to make a lasting impact on the game. Next I'd place the British Open, both because of what it represents in the evolution of golf and because of the completeness of playing skills it requires—not to mention its true internationalism. (The fact that both these events are national champion-

ships also influences me in rating them first and second.) It's difficult to chose between the Masters and the PGA for third and fourth places because they are so different in character, but it's my feeling that the PGA is fourth in most people's minds only because it is fourth in the playing order. If it were switched with the Masters, I think there would be a whole different attitude toward it. But this is all academic, really. They are all great events, they all occupy an indelible place in golf's fabric, and I'll take any one of them I can win at any time.

Here's one of those young-man-makes-good shots from the family album, taken at the end of 1963. The trophies, from left to right, represent my Amateur, Open, Masters, PGA and World Cup (then Canada Cup) team and individual wins.

Augusta '65

Well, it seems I'm still going with the throwing bit, only this time it's the ball instead of the hat. And, of course, since I'm so cool and controlled and emotionless, it's all been worked out and precisely calculated coming up the eighteenth fairway!

Seriously, I threw the ball because the galleries had been so super to me at this Masters compared with the one in 1963 that I felt I just wanted to give them something. It wasn't much to give, but it was the only way I could show them a little of how I felt at that moment.

This was the record year, of course, and obviously I played some of the best golf of my life that week. It remains one of the most memorable times of my life. I shot 67-71-64-69—271 to finish a record nine shots ahead of Arnold Palmer and Gary Player and also break Ben Hogan's seventy-two-hole Masters record by three strokes (Ray Floyd tied my 271 in 1976).

Funnily enough, this low round of 64 (still tied with Lloyd Mangrum, Maurice Bembridge and Hale Irwin for the course

OFFICIAL SCORE CARD

HOLE	1	2	3	4	5	6	7	8	9	Out	10	11	12	13	14	15	16	17	18	In	Totals
YARDAGE	400	555	355	220	450	190	365	530	400	3555	470	445	155	475	420	520	190	400	420	3555	6950
PAR	4	5	4	3	4	3	4	5	4	36	4	4	3	5	4	5	3	4	4	36	72
PLAYER	4	4	4	2	4	2	3	4	4	31	4	4	3	4	4	4	2	4	4	33	64

I have checked my score hole by hole.

Player Signature — *Jack Nicklaus*
Jack Nicklaus

Attest *Dan Sikes Jr*
Saturday APR 10 1965

record) was actually the easiest of the tournament because I was playing so well. Both the weather and the course conditions were perfect for scoring all four days, and the way I was playing in the Saturday round, I really didn't take 100 percent advantage of them—I could have shot three or four shots better. But that's the way with every great round you play, and I'm certainly not complaining—just being realistic.

Anyone who attended the Masters regularly in those days could not but be saddened, amid all that life and vigor and color, by the continual decline in Bob Jones's health, evident in this picture when compared with the one in 1963 on page 61.

The happy people on the couch with the author are (right to left) Arnold Palmer, Gary Player and low amateur Downing Gray. Cliff Roberts is opposite me, next to the fireplace. The location is the basement of the Butler Cabin, and the occasion the post-Masters TV interview. Seeing Gary, Arnie and myself like this reminds me of how much golf we'd then been playing together in "Big Three" television matches. Spending so much time with these fellows for those events was what really brought home Arnold's graciousness and charm as a man and an appreciation of the enormous effort Gary had put out to become a world-class athlete. We all became very good friends over those years, despite trying to beat one another's brains out every time we teed up together.

Augusta '66

This win made me the first and so far [through 1978] the only golfer to successfully defend a Masters title. It was an extremely hard week for me, and I counted myself very fortunate to get into the playoff with Tommy Jacobs and Gay Brewer with an even-par score of 288.

For a variety of reasons, I hadn't prepared quite as thoroughly earlier in the year as had become customary; and then on the eve of the first round, I suffered a deep personal loss when Bob Barton, one of the closest friends I've ever had, was killed along with his wife and another couple from Columbus while flying down in a private plane to watch the tournament. Only Barbara's wise counsel finally got me to play at all, but the way I played for the four regulation rounds was the worst I've ever performed in a major and still won. Sheer perseverance was all that kept me in there, plus the fact that it was one of those years when no one seemed to want to win—seventeen players held or shared the lead at some point in the tournament.

This picture is of my third shot at the last hole of the play-off, and it's the last place I should have been at that point. The grass there was heavily trampled by the galleries, and there was just no shot except to somehow bumble the ball and hope it would roll up onto the green. Actually, I used a putter and managed to get down in two (this was one of only two majors, incidentally, that I've won with a putter different from the one I use today;

the other was the U.S. Open in 1967). But the situation was typical of the scrappy golf I played.

Here's a key shot in the play-off—the longest birdie putt I made, a twenty-five-footer at eleven, which increased my lead to the two shots I eventually won by. And that fellow up in the air is Willie Peterson, the greatest high jumper in golf! Willie's caddied for me in every Masters I've played except the first one, in 1959. As regulars know, you really don't have to watch me at Augusta to tell how I'm doing—just Willie! He really is a great reactor; the only problem is that he often gets a little ahead of himself and starts leaping around when he just *thinks* the ball is going in the hole. If it had as often as he's jumped, I'd have won fifteen Masters, not five.

Just a nice moment with Barbara coming off the eighteenth green. Excepting 1963, when Steve was born three days after the tournament ended, she has been with me at every Masters but one since we were married in 1960, and I don't think she's ever missed a shot I've hit in those tournaments in all that time.

green jacket. I think my answer was, "Quite honestly, Mr. Roberts, no, I wouldn't!" But he said, "Come on, I think you'll enjoy yourself," and he was right. Spending the next two days with him seeing the Masters from totally different perspectives was one of the nicest experiences I ever had.

Muirfield '66

"If at first you don't succeed, try, try again." That was pretty much the early story of my British Open efforts, and it's become that way again recently. Once I became a professional, I won the U.S. Open on my first attempt and the Masters and PGA the second time I played in them. It took me five years to win my first British Open, and through 1977 I've gone seven years since my second victory. Better than anything else, I think, my placings show how resolutely I've stuck to the old "try, try again" adage. Since 1963, excluding the two wins, I have finished third, second, tied twelfth, second, tied second, sixth, tied fifth, second, fourth, third, tied third, tied second, second. Oh, well, I suppose I can always fall back on another old saw: "Patience is a virtue."

Actually, I'm as proud of my first British Open win as anything I've achieved in golf. The reason is that I did a number of things at Muirfield that I wasn't supposed to be capable of doing at that time. Number one, because of my high shots, was to play in the wind. There was never a howl-

Here, for contrast, is an example of how golf keeps everyone down to size.

I'd embarrassed myself mightily by missing the cut in the U.S. Open in 1963 after winning it the previous year. Darned if I didn't do the same thing again in the Masters in 1967 after winning *two* years in a row. Normally, I'd leave the scene pretty fast in a situation like that, but Cliff Roberts, driving the cart here, came to me and asked me if I'd like to ride around the course with him the next day and perhaps stay on through Sunday too, to present the

ing gale that week, but it was definitely somewhat more than drafty most of the time. Number two was to win when distance was "neutralized" by narrow fairways and heavy rough. The fairways at Muirfield that year were certainly among the slenderest I have ever encountered, and the rough quite definitely was the most penal I've ever experienced anywhere in the world—waist high and waving at you like Kansas wheat on the majority of the holes. (Seems the British were scared some of the American howitzers would make mincemeat of these very proud links given windless but holding conditions, and they tricked them up as a defense against that possibility. With a course of such total balance and integrity, that, in my view, was a mistake. Obviously, the Royal and Ancient Golf Club thought so too, upon reflection, because there was no such gimmickry when Muirfield was next used for the British Open, in 1972.) Number three, because of my four previous failures to do so, was to win in Britain.

Perhaps here I can allow myself what may sound like a less than modest comment in regard not only to this victory but to many of the others I have enjoyed around the world. To the average fan, the most impressive aspects of my game are my shotmaking capabilities and my distance. To me, they are not. I'm a powerful enough golfer, yes, and generally a competent shotmaker, but I'm certainly no better in these departments than five or ten other guys playing tournament golf at any given time. Where I believe my strongest suits lie are in the mind, not the body. I am a reasonably intelligent individual, and at golf I have almost always been able to apply my intelligence ahead of my emotions and my muscles. Very early on in my career, fortunately, my intelligence told me that once you possess the shots, two factors above all others will determine your success at golf. One is the degree of reality you can apply to the game. The other is the degree of patience you can sustain, especially when you are under the pressure of either winning or losing something immensely important to you.

My first British Open win was a fine example of these factors. I did not like the way the course had been set up, but after the first shock and disappointment, I was able to accept the reality of it emotionally rather than spending my time complaining to myself or others and wishing for something different. The practical decision arising out of that was to play entirely for position with irons off most of the tees (I used the driver only seventeen times during the entire seventy-two holes). As for the prospect of being up to my navel in hay anytime I missed a fairway, by the time the tournament started, all it had done was fix my mind on the need for patience. Losing my temper would simply have made any given situation worse. Thus, right from the start, I was able to look at the event not in terms of my hole-by-hole or even my day-by-day score, but as a seventy-two-hole contest within which there would inevitably be considerable fluctuations of fortune for all involved, myself included. It proved a win-

ning attitude then, as it has many times since.

The picture here shows this strategy in action. Both the length and the fairway bunkering of the last hole at Muirfield tempt a long hitter to go with the driver. I knew I'd have a difficult long-iron approach if I drove with less. But I had made a basic decision about how to avoid the wheat, and it had gotten me this far needing a par to win, so I stuck with it. That's a one-iron I've just hit.

This is the rough I was talking about. Correction: This is the *semi*rough. The real stuff was about a foot higher.

70

I'd just walked off the eighteenth green here. Both Barb and I were obviously ecstatic.

There it is, the oldest trophy in golf, finally on its way for a spell on the Nicklaus mantelpiece. It was because this win and golf course meant so much to me that I named the area where my own golf club is located, in Columbus, Muirfield Village. (Tying in with that, we also used the outline of this trophy as the centerpiece of the club's crest.) Actually, the course itself is called the Memorial Course after the tournament held there annually honoring the game's past great players. Unfortunately, it has come to be called just "Muirfield," which makes it look as though we simply stole the exact name from the Scots. That wasn't the intention at all.

Baltusrol '67

Someone worked out in 1976 that my average placing in the majors as a pro up to that year had been fifth in the Masters, a shade over fifth in both the British Open and the PGA, and a little worse than twelfth in the U.S. Open. That's a fair reflection of which of these championships is the most difficult to win, at least in my case.

The U.S. Open has become tougher the older I've gotten, which doesn't surprise me a bit when I relate my strength in my late teens and early and mid twenties to my strength today. As everyone who follows golf closely knows, the Open has traditionally been the one American tournament in which really heavy rough is a constant playing factor. As a youngster and a young man, that never really bothered me, because I was long enough to be able to hit middle- and short-irons to most of the greens and strong enough to tear the ball out of the tall grass with those clubs on most of the occasions when I missed fairways. Also, having played so many events on USGA-prepared courses as an amateur, I was a pretty straight driver when I first turned pro. Rough, however, was rarely much of a factor on most of the PGA-tour courses we played in my early pro days, so, with accuracy less of a premium than distance, I gradually became a more and more crooked driver between about 1963 and the early seventies. That's been corrected in recent years, but now, of course, I don't have quite the bulldozing power I used to have from Open-type rough.

71

This was probably my optimum period for both accuracy and strength: twenty-seven years old and winning my second U.S. Open, at Baltusrol. This twenty-two-foot birdie putt on the final hole set a new Open record of 275, one better than Ben Hogan's total at Riviera in 1948. You can tell what Arnie, who was second by four shots, thought about it all from the expression on his face. (But the "army" seems to have been still hoping for some sort of miracle—note the "Go, Arnie, Go" sign aloft in the left background.)

I came into this championship having shot a 62 in my last practice round and feeling just great, and I played the golf I expected to with 71-67-72-65. Once again, Deane Beman had made a contribution by suggesting the previous week that a different putter might ease the woes I'd been suffering on the greens and by getting one from a friend of his, Fred Mueller. It was a center-shafted Bullseye model that Fred had painted white to prevent sun glare from the brass head, and it worked like a dream at Baltusrol and pretty well for a couple of months after that. But eventually the magic left it, and I switched again to the flanged-blade putter I'd used for most of the time until then. After finally deciding it was the "puttee," not the putter, that really mattered, I haven't changed putters again in ten years.

Friends tell me I've always been miraculously lucky with weather both on the

golf course and in other things I do. This was certainly true at Baltusrol, because it went black as night and pelted down with rain immediately after I finished. Obviously, neither Barb nor I cared a hoot at that point.

St. Andrews '70

These, I can assure you, were not contrived emotions! I still feel bad about nearly denting poor old Doug Sanders by flinging my putter in the air, but the action came out of my sheer uncontrollable joy at winning my first major in three years—and at winning it at St. Andrews.

Winning "*the* Open" at the Old Course had been a dream of mine ever since I began to play the game. The ambition had grown stronger the more conscious I became not only of what St. Andrews represented in golf, but of how important such an achievement is in the attitude of the entire golfing world toward a man's record. Rightly or wrongly, like Bobby Jones, I felt a victory here in the cradle of golf was critical to being regarded as at least a "complete" golfer and probably essential to ever being rated the best of one's time. I'd been second to an inspired Tony Lema at my only other try here six years previously, and with the seven- or eight-course rotation of the British Open, I knew there wouldn't be too many opportunities in the future. I'd almost started packing to go home as Doug came to the last green of regulation play needing two putts to win, and I've never felt sorrier for a fellow than when he missed that short second putt. But for me the play-off was a heaven-sent opportunity, and I've rarely been closer to heaven than I was here at the end of it.

Yes, sometimes the rough can be extremely deep in Britain! Actually, I'm playing out of a bunker here, not a wheat field as it seems. But note that Doug has a wood in his hand, whereas I have a wedge, a nice comment on some of my play that week.

"I just want to touch it once!" said Doug at the presentation. Considering what he must have been going through emotionally, there couldn't have been a more gracious loser.

What turned out to be a most enjoyable week had started with a very enjoyable evening—a dinner given by the Royal and Ancient Golf Club in their famous old clubhouse for past British Open champions. Standing, left to right, are Arthur Havers (1923), Gene Sarazen (1932), Richard Burton (1939), Fred Daly (1947), Roberto de Vicenzo (1967), Arnold Palmer (1961–62), Kel Nagle (1960), Bobby Locke (1949–50, 1952, 1957), Henry Cotton (1934, 1937, 1948) and Peter Thomson (1954–55–56, 1958, 1965). Kneeling, left to right, are Densmore Shute (1933), Bob Charles (1963), Max Faulkner (1951), my-self (1966, 1970), Tony Jacklin (1969) and Gary Player (1959, 1968, 1974).

By her choice, Barb walks all of every round with me at the tournaments she attends—all the majors and most of the other events I play when the children are out of school. She is pictured (page 76) at St. Andrews in 1970. I've always known she rarely misses shots, but I never realized until I saw this picture for the first time in preparing this book that she sometimes has less than total confidence in my ability to execute them.

Seriously, apart from the crossed fin-

75

gers, this is pretty typical of her golf-watching form. Many of the writers believe she's the world champion at routing a course so as to achieve the maximum visibility for the minimum amount of legwork and crowd crush. In fact, when a new course needs to be cased, a number of the guys actually follow her to be sure of mapping the best vantage points.

Palm Beach Gardens '71

Usually, we rent a house near the course for the week of a major championship so that we can enjoy some privacy and also so that we can stay as close to our everyday family life as possible. This PGA Championship was the one time I've not had to do that—it's the one major I've won as a commuter from my own home. Gary Player was our houseguest for the week, and with the then PGA National course only ten minutes away, everybody had a lot of fun.

This was a big event for me in quite a number of ways. For one thing, because of special scheduling circumstances, it was played in February, making it the first instead of the last major championship of the year. I had by then gone four years with only one win in the majors (the British Open seven months previously), and I badly wanted to get firmly back onto that particular trail. Additionally, a win here would make me the first golfer to take all four majors twice. Also, despite living in Florida since the mid-sixties, I had never won a professional individual tournament on 100 percent Bermuda greens (not overseeded with a softer winter grass). Arnold Palmer and I had won the 1966 National Team Championship here, but with all the experience I had since gained of Bermuda grass and of Florida wind, it bugged me never to have won individually under home-style conditions. Given the length and severity of the then PGA National East Course, I figured this might be the time to put all those matters to rights, and so it proved.

With the season so young, I had not been putting well up to then, but the ever helpful Deane Beman fixed that over at

the house the evening before the first round by telling me to complete my backstroke. Here, I've just holed out on the last green, finishing seven under par for a two-shot margin over Billy Casper.

This was my opening drive in the final round—that's the trophy on the table. I was swinging the club particularly well that week, as an incident in practice seemed to exemplify. Playing with Gary, Tom Weiskopf and Tony Jacklin, I caught a bunker on the right of the twelfth fairway off the tee. This hole is 510 yards long and it was playing into the wind that day, but we had a couple of dollars on the game and I thought I'd go for all the marbles. So I took a three-wood and knocked it out of the sand onto the green about 250 yards away. All three of the guys were stunned—they thought it was one of the most unbelievable shots they'd ever seen. I treated it nonchalantly, of course, but secretly I was inclined to agree: the margin for error is so fractional on such a shot that there has to be some luck involved, no matter how good the swing.

Here's my old friend Bob Hope making the presentation. I'll have more to say about Bob later, but the fact that he was there for the final day reminds me how amazingly energetic he is—he's the hardest-working septuagenarian and certainly the heaviest traveler I've ever known.

I launched Hathaway patterned golf shirts that week. I'd been associated with this fine shirt company for quite a while; in fact, I was closely involved in designing the shirt that has since become a staple on the market under the "Golf Classic" brand. (The open half sleeves and the dress-type collar with a long placket to give enough weight to hold the collar down were my ideas.) Just prior to the tournament, the Hathaway fellows had given me some beautifully patterned shirts, but said they weren't planning to market them because they wouldn't sell. I said, "Poppycock," or a ruder equivalent, and wore one every day except the last. The following week, Hathaway had more than two hundred calls from retailers all over the country for those shirts, and they've done fabulously with patterns ever since.

Augusta '72

Looks like some sort of vaudeville act! Actually, it was our reaction to a good-sized birdie putt on the sixteenth green in the first round. I finished with a 68 to lead and stayed in front for the rest of the tournament, eventually winning by three shots with a 286. I was the only player under par, and the win enabled me to join

78

modern Grand Slam in mind for quite a while, of course, and I think this was the year that proved what I've always said about it, which is that it is "a possibility but not a probability." The possibility this time ended when Lee Trevino chipped in at the seventeenth hole of the final round of the British Open at Muirfield, placing me second by one shot despite a closing 66. But my winning the first two and then coming so close in the third did convince me that taking all four in one year isn't beyond the bounds of possibility.

Here's Willie, resting for some more high jumps. Actually, I'd kept him waiting a while for practice and he'd fallen asleep.

Arnold Palmer as the only four-time Masters champions.

With so much golf still ahead of me, I hate to say this was my best year ever, but there's a possibility it might turn out to be that way. Prior to the Masters I'd won the Crosby and the Doral Eastern, and I went on to win the U.S. Open, the Westchester, the Liggett & Myers U.S. Professional Match Play, and the Disney World Open —seven wins out of nineteen starts on the home tour, plus a then record $320,542 in prize money. I matched the number of wins the following year in fewer starts (eighteen), but my major-championship record was inferior—just the PGA Championship as opposed to 1972's Masters and U.S. Open.

By the beginning of 1972, I'd had a

In the early sixties, Jack Grout decided he'd had enough of cold Midwestern winters and left Scioto for the pro job at La Gorce in Miami Beach. A big operation like that can become tough duty as a fellow gets older, and I was delighted when we built Muirfield Village to be able to persuade him to come back to Columbus as our teacher-in-chief and pro emeritus.

Although I generally don't need to call on Jack at the majors if I've prepared properly, he likes to attend many of them, and it's a comfort to have him on hand. Here we are at Augusta in 1972. He always attended the Masters as part of what came to be known, because of a certain amount of evening festivity, as "Charlie's Gang" —my dad's group. Since my father died, Jack has come to Augusta each year with my uncle, Frank Nicklaus, and a group of old family friends. Hope I can look that young and sharp when I'm Jack's age.

This was the first Masters that my eldest son, Jackie, attended. Here we are with Barb just after the tournament ended. He was ten then and just beginning to get seriously into golf. Five years later, he shot an 80 on his first round of the Augusta course, playing from the back tees with two members and myself the week before the tournament.

I insisted this picture be in the book as a counterpoint to the one taken nine years previously in the same circumstances (page 60). The difference is about thirty pounds! Helping me on with the green jacket is 1971 champion Charlie Coody.

Pebble Beach '72

Having won the Amateur at Pebble Beach in 1961 and my second Crosby there five months previously, and loving the course so much, I definitely felt I had an edge going into this U.S. Open. Obviously, with the Masters already in my satchel and those Grand Slam thoughts in mind, I had prepared very thoroughly. Another encouraging factor was that I could use my left-to-right game almost entirely, Pebble Beach being far more susceptible to this shape of shot than any other.

Everything worked out as planned, and I won by three strokes over Bruce Crampton with a two-over-par 290—indicative of how tough the course played, after the usual USGA-Open preparation treatment and in what seemed like a continually rising and drying wind. Since I'd already won the PGA Championship and the Masters, this win put me the closest I've yet been to holding all four major titles at the same time.

Here's the shot that locked things up for me—a one-iron dead into the wind to the seventeenth hole on the last round that hit the pin and finished an inch or two away from a "one." Strangely enough, of the three one-iron shots that really stand out in my mind (the others are the approach to the last hole at Baltusrol in 1967 and the shot to the fifteenth at Augusta in the last round of the 1975 Masters), I've always felt that I made the poorest swing on this one. My tempo and timing had been marvelous all that week at Pebble, and that's what saved me here. Setting up to the ball, I was very conscious of the ocean on the left of the green, and going back I could feel myself making an instinctive reaction to that, shutting the clubface slightly and swinging a little too much to the inside. Fortunately, when your timing is as good as mine was that week, you can sometimes adjust coming down for little backswing errors like those, and that's what I did here.

A good analyst of form would be able to tell from the amount of extension in this picture that I have delayed the release fractionally in order not to let the clubhead turn over too quickly and hook the ball into the ocean. The result, a very slight "blocking" of the shot, produced a nice low, drilling-type flight dead on the stick. (Coincidentally, I thought I'd hit exactly the same shot here when I needed two pars to tie for the 1977 PGA Championship, except with a four-iron and a better swing. Unfortunately, although the ball landed in the middle of the green, it took a bad bounce and ended in a spot just off the green from which it was virtually impossible to get up and down in two.)

Here's one of the greatest places in golf —the eighteenth tee at Pebble Peach. Although it hasn't always been too kind to me, I also love the entire hole—in fact, I'd choose it as the prettiest and one of the most demanding par 5s anywhere.

I see Jackie made two majors that year! He's listening as I talked to President Nixon, whose custom it was at that time to call the winners of big sports events. I'd met President Nixon but never had the chance to play golf with him, as I have quite a few times with his successor, President Ford.

Jackie, incidentally, shot a 99 from the back tees at Pebble Beach the week before the Open—and that after almost giving up golf permanently a couple of days previously. We'd gone to play Spyglass, and on the first hole he got mad and slammed the club down. I told him that if he did not start behaving like a gentleman, the next place he'd be visiting would be the clubhouse. When we got to the green, he let go with another little temper display, so off we went to the clubhouse— only one hole was played that day.

I might add I had one—and only one —similar experience with my father at about the same age, and I'm glad to say that's all it took for Jackie to get *his* head straight about how golf is played.

Canterbury '73

Obviously, all my major-championship wins have been tremendous thrills, but here's one that will always be very special —my fourteenth if, as most people in golf do, you count the two U.S. Amateur wins. The event was the PGA Championship, and I won by four shots over Bruce Crampton with a seven-under-par 277. Here's my reaction to a good-sized birdie putt on the sixteenth hole that I felt wrapped things up for me.

84

Naturally, Bobby Jones's total of thirteen majors had been very much in my mind for years and was particularly prominent in my thinking this week. I'd like however, to make a comment about Jones's achievement that I think is important. When I won my fourteenth title here at Canterbury I did not, as I see it, actually "break" Jones's record in the sense of taking anything away from him. If there cannot be a valid comparison between one golfer's period and another's—as there cannot between Jones's and mine—then no valid comparison can be made between their playing records. The majors in Jones's time were the Amateur and Open championships of Great Britain and the United States. He won thirteen of those playing as an amateur, within a period of six years, in an average of fewer than four tournaments a year, while obtaining an extensive education and starting a successful law practice. The majors by my time had become the Masters, the U.S. and British Opens and the PGA Championship. I have now won fourteen of those as a professional, over a thirteen-year period, entering an average of twenty events a year, while concentrating primarily on tournament golf. In that light, I think any direct comparison is pointless. In my view, *both* totals are records, and each should stand independently until they are broken in the same tournaments and by comparable types of players. It's my conviction that Jones's record never will be broken, whereas I'm sure mine will be someday.

85

Canterbury remains special not only for the "fourteenth," but because we had all the family there that week—and very much involved, as you can see here! This is Gary, our second youngest, who was four at the time. I'd just putted out on the last green in the third round, and he was standing in the gallery with Barbara. "Hey! There's my dad!" he yelled, and ran out before Barb could stop him and jumped into my arms. He also made the press tent as much as I did that week, insisting on going with me for every interview (free soda was the big attraction, I think).

This has long been one of my favorite pictures of Barbara and me together. Playing in Ohio meant we had a lot of old friends around, which made it a special week.

It was also, incidentally, the first major I had won in my original home state.

Augusta '75

Here's the most enjoyable moment of the tournament I've enjoyed the most to date—the forty-five-footer on sixteen that proved to be the key shot in winning a record fifth Masters. It was the longest critical putt I've yet holed in a major, and oddly enough I thought I might make it even before I stepped up to the ball, which doesn't happen very often from that distance.

Actually, my playing partner, Tom Watson, inadvertently helped me quite a lot here by going in the water a couple of times and thus causing me to wait a while before putting. You can see the fifteenth hole very clearly from the sixteenth green, and Tom's problems gave me the chance to watch both Tom Weiskopf and Johnny Miller make birdies there, placing them, respectively, one ahead of me and one behind. Realizing then that I couldn't simply lag the ball, I started thinking about similar putts I'd made from the same general area of this sixteenth green. Suddenly I had the feeling that this putt was makable too.

You can tell from the first picture that both Willie and I thought the ball was going in the moment it crested the hill. And, as the other pictures show, my reaction when it did was obviously among the most exuberant of my career.

Thinking, I suppose, about the pressure all of us were under in this incredibly close and hard-fought finish, people are often surprised when I talk about how much sheer fun it all was. Well, the fact of

the matter is that the tougher and closer the competition, the more I enjoy golf. Winning by easy margins may offer other kinds of satisfaction, but it's nowhere nearly as *enjoyable* as battling it out shot by shot right down to the wire.

I might add that this holds true even when I don't win, because the next two most enjoyable tournaments I've ever played were the 1977 Masters and British Open. Even though I lost both to Tom Watson, each to me was the very essence of what sport is all about. It's great to win, but it's also great fun just to be in the thick of any truly well- and hard-fought contest against opponents you respect, whatever the outcome.

Arnold Palmer and I played together in the third round. As usual, we suffered from the pairing, both shooting our highest rounds of the week. We agreed beforehand, as we have in the past, to try our hardest not to let playing together affect us, but the "shoot-out" mentality of the press and the fans makes that very difficult once you get onto the course. We were very much at the head of things starting out this day, but both of us struggled, Arnie to the point of negating his best chance at Augusta in some years. Perhaps if the writers and fans realized that they actually reduce both our chances by being so partisan, they'd cool it a little.

During the 1952 Masters, Ben Hogan, the defending champion, hosted a dinner at the club for all the previous winners of the tournament. Nine of the eleven eligible players attended, and they enjoyed themselves so much that Ben suggested forming a Masters Club and having a similar affair each year. Everyone agreed and also voted to extend honorary membership to Bob Jones and Cliff Roberts.

Since then, the Masters Club dinner has been held on the Tuesday evening prior to the tournament and always gets a fine turnout. It's all very informal, with a lot of banter over cocktails and dinner, a few

words from the defending champion (who traditionally picks up the tab), and then a couple of Sam Snead's hilarious stories to round off the festivities.

The primary purpose of the evening is simply to enjoy one another's company, but as Cliff Roberts said on numerous occasions, it has also proved a fine forum for ideas for improving the tournament, which is the continuing preoccupation of everyone involved with the Masters. Bill Lane, the new tournament chairman, has been invited to join the club now that both Bob and Cliff are no longer with us.

Here's the last dinner I hosted, in 1976, with twenty-one of the twenty-four members present. Clockwise, around the room from me are Sam Snead, Gene Sarazen, Gary Player, Art Wall, Gay Brewer, Henry Picard, George Archer, Jack Burke, Billy Casper, Jimmy Demaret, Charlie Coody, Bob Goalby, Doug Ford, Herman Keiser, Ralph Guldahl, Claude Harmon, Tommy Aaron, Arnold Palmer, Byron Nelson and Clifford Roberts.

I get this sort of kiss when I win. Otherwise, it's a peck on the cheek.

Firestone '75

Firestone was the site of the last of my major-championship wins to date—but I hope not the final one.

Firestone had been very good to me over the years, with four firsts in the old four-man World Series and one American Golf Classic win, and I looked forward to being on virtually "home" ground there for the PGA, together with the family and many of our Ohio friends. As a writer put it the following week, I "lurked in the shadows for a couple of rounds," then took the lead on the third day and held on to it throughout the fourth for an eventual two-shot margin over Bruce Crampton (this was the fourth time in four years that Bruce had been runner-up to me in a major).

If Firestone has a failing, it is a feeling of "sameness" about a lot of holes because of the similarity of the overall terrain. But there's one hole I'm unlikely ever to forget after what happened in the Saturday round. This is the sixteenth, the 625-yard par 5 known locally as "The Monster." Assuming the tee would be far back, I'd automatically taken the driver from my caddie, Angelo, as we left the fifteenth green, and he had then moved on down the fairway. When I got to the tee, I found it had been moved some thirty yards forward, calling ideally for a three-wood. Rather than haul Angelo back, I decided to just cozy the tee shot with the driver. Typically, I then hit it very hard and dead left into a water hazard. Dropping out under a one-shot penalty, I attempted next to play my third shot safely down the fairway with a six-iron, but hit a hard "flyer" that ended up close behind a thirty-foot tree in the right rough 137 yards from the pin, which was set only a few feet beyond the lake fronting the green. The shot looked next to impossible, and I knew I was staring at an eight if I missed it, but for some reason I had a strong impulse to go for it. So I took a big cut with a nine-iron and, lo and behold, when I ducked out from behind the trees there was the ball sitting thirty feet beyond the pin. Naturally, the putt had to be holed to fully restore my dignity. When it dropped, I think I accepted the applause with an appropriate degree of blaséness.

Actually, it was one of the dumbest holes from tee to green I've ever played in strategical terms—and definitely one of the finest pars I've ever made.

Next to 1972, this year was the closest I've yet come to the modern Grand Slam. You have to win them one by one in order, of course, which disqualified my chances after the U.S. Open at Medinah. But looking back at the end of this final major of the year, I realized how close it had been, with a two-shot loss at Medinah and a one-shot defeat in the British Open at Carnoustie.

But you can't live by "ifs," and I was quite happy to be able to say about the PGA, as this picture suggests, "At least this one's mine, fellows!"

...And Two of Many That Slipped Away

The Masters, Augusta National, 1977. I'd just played one of the finest rounds of my life—and had it matched shot for shot by a golfer who just wouldn't crack. Here, I'm doubtless thinking over what happened on the final hole as we await the prize presentation.

Basically, my error was to expect Tom Watson to make a mistake coming down to the wire. I'd played in the Masters often enough to know what the probabilities are in certain situations, and I figured that

there was an excellent chance a par at eighteen would win or at least get me into a play-off. I'd hit a good tee shot and had just finished programming myself to hit a solid six-iron for the middle of the green and two putts when the roar at seventeen signified that Tom had birdied. I wasn't expecting that, and it jarred me. Now I'd have to try to get close enough to the pin for a single putt, which required a soft six-iron—a seven wouldn't be enough to get me there—and a complete reprogramming of mind and muscle dead against the high flow of adrenalin I was obviously experiencing.

For one of the few times in my life at a moment like that, I wasn't able to reprogram totally, and I hit a bad shot—a fat shot instead of a soft one. This was a mental error, which is the kind I've always hated most in golf, and my reaction here tells exactly how I felt about it.

The British Open, Turnberry, 1977. Well, now I've just played *two* of the greatest rounds of my life and lost to one equally as good and one better—and to the same fellow who did it to me at the Masters.

Seriously, there is no question that Tom Watson played the better golf from tee to green that week. I hung in there with some good recovery shots and generally solid putting, but my driving left an awful lot to be desired. Here we are on the last green, following which I received some nice compliments on my graciousness as a loser. Taking the attitude, as I always have, that golf is only a game helps a lot at moments like these.

Incidentally, my 269 in this tournament was my lowest-ever score in a major. Tom's 268, of course, is the "majors record," and one that should stand for a while, I'd guess.

Chapter 4
On and Off
the Fairway

On and Off the Fairway

U.S. tournaments entered 1962–77: 321
Total victories through 1977: 79 world-
 wide, 63 U.S.

1962 (26 U.S. events)

U.S. Open
Seattle Open
Portland Open
World Series of Golf
 Rookie of Year

1963 (21 U.S. events)

Palm Springs Classic
Masters
Tournament of Champions
PGA Championship
World Series of Golf
Sahara Invitational
World Cup team (with Arnold Palmer)
World Cup individual

1964 (24 U.S. events)

Portland Open
Tournament of Champions
Phoenix Open
Whitemarsh Open
Australian Open
World Cup team (with Arnold Palmer)

World Cup individual
 Leading money-winner: $113,284
 Lowest stroke average: 69.9

1965 (24 U.S. events)

Portland Open
Masters
Memphis Open
Thunderbird Classic
Philadelphia Classic
 Leading money-winner: $140,752
 Lowest stroke average: 70.1

1966 (19 U.S. events)

Masters
British Open
Sahara Invitational
National Team Championship (with Arnold
 Palmer)
World Cup team (with Arnold Palmer)

1967 (21 U.S. events)

Crosby National Pro-Am
U.S. Open

Western Open
Westchester Classic
World Series of Golf
Sahara Invitational
World Cup team (with Arnold Palmer)
    Leading money-winner: $188,988
    PGA Player of the Year

1968 (22 U.S. events)

Western Open
American Golf Classic
Australian Open

1969 (19 U.S. events)

Andy Williams–San Diego Open
Kaiser Invitational
Sahara Invitational
    Ryder Cup team member

1970 (22 U.S. events)

Byron Nelson Classic
British Open
National Team Championship (with Arnold
    Palmer)
World Series of Golf
Piccadilly World Match Play (England)

1971 (18 U.S. events)

Tournament of Champions
Byron Nelson Classic
PGA Championship
National Team Championship (with Arnold
    Palmer)
Disney World Open
Australian Open
Australian Dunlop
World Cup team (with Lee Trevino)

World Cup individual
    Leading money-winner: $244,490
    Lowest stroke average: 70.08
    Ryder Cup team member

1972 (19 U.S. events)

Crosby National Pro-Am
Doral Eastern Open
Masters
U.S. Open
Westchester Classic
U.S. Professional Match-Play Championship
Disney World Open
    Leading money-winner: $320,542
    Lowest stroke average: 70.23
    PGA Player of the Year
    Golf Writers' Player of the Year

1973 (18 U.S. events)

Crosby National Pro-Am
Tournament of Champions
Greater New Orleans Open
Atlanta Classic
PGA Championship
Ohio Kings Island Open
Disney World Open
World Cup team (with Johnny Miller)
    Leading money-winner: $308,362
    Lowest stroke average: 69.81
    PGA Player of the Year
    Ryder Cup team member

1974 (18 U.S. events)

Tournament Players Championship
Hawaiian Open
    Lowest stroke average: 70.06

1975 (16 U.S. events)

Doral Eastern Open
Heritage Classic

Masters
PGA Championship
World Open
Australian Open
    Leading money-winner: $298,149
    Lowest stroke average: 69.87
    PGA Player of the Year
    Golf Writers' Player of the Year
    Ryder Cup team member
    Bobby Jones Award (for distinguished
        sportsmanship)

1976 (16 U.S. events)

Tournament Players Championship
World Series of Golf

Australian Open
    Leading money-winner: $266,438
    Lowest stroke average: 70.17
    PGA Player of the Year
    Golf Writers' Player of the Year (jointly
        with Jerry Pate)

1977 (18 U.S. events)

Jackie Gleason Inverrary Classic
Tournament of Champions
Memorial Tournament
    Ryder Cup team member

A Nice Bonus

Tough as it is, I've always liked Firestone because of how hard it requires you to think before you hit the ball: it's one of the few courses we play on tour, beyond those set up for major championships, that offer absolutely no "breather" holes. Here's a happy moment following my first win there, in the 1962 World Series of Golf—a nice bonus to end a fellow's rookie year. Sharing it are my father-in-law, Stanley Bash (center), and my dad, Charlie Nicklaus. Stanley, a high school mathematics teacher by profession, knew very little about golf before I appeared in his daughter's life, but very quickly became—and remains—one of my keenest supporters.

À La Française

Here's the first of four Canada Cups/World Cups Arnie and I won together, at the then recently opened St. Nom de la Bretèche Golf Club on the outskirts of Paris in 1963. This isn't a fuzzy picture—fog delayed the tournament and eventually forced a reduction of the final round to nine holes.

I believe I'm right in saying that golf in France got a great boost from this event, leading to further big tournaments and an upsurge in both golf course construction and playing standards over the next several years, and I know the World Cup has had similar effects in many other countries. It certainly is a different event from the regular run of pro tournaments and obviously an extremely worthwhile one in terms of building golf around the world. I've played in it seven times all told and am proud to have done so.

A Favorite Place

How you play there makes a difference in how you feel about a lot of places, but here's one I'll always love, win or lose: the first and eighteenth fairways of the Old Course at St. Andrews, as seen here from the footbridge over the Swilken Burn, with the Royal and Ancient clubhouse in the left background. The year was 1964, and I was getting my yardages on my first practice round for the British Open. I finished second to Tony Lema, who won despite leaving himself almost no time for practice and in the worst winds I think any of us has ever experienced in a major championship.

Weight Match

The first pro title I defended successfully was the Tournament of Champions, in 1964. Fittingly for Las Vegas, the prize money that year was paid in silver dollars—twelve thousand of them. Needless to say, they just about matched my weight at that time!

This tournament has been very good to me, with five wins through 1977, and I'm often asked how it is I've done so well in it, coming as it does immediately after either the high of winning the Masters or the low of failing to win it. The answer really is very simple. Depending on the Masters result, I'm definitely psychologically either way up or way down at the time of the T of C, and always pretty tired. But I'm also in good playing shape as the result of the preparation I've done for Augusta. As the record shows, this sort of carry-over has happened to me quite a

number of times during my pro career, and it has become one of the reasons why, as the years have passed, I've been more and more careful about pacing my play.

If I have one "secret," it is proper preparation for the events that mean the most to me, and I don't intend to forgo that, whatever the pressures upon me to play more.

Out Cold Again

Steven Charles had joined us on April 11, 1963, and we became a family of five with Nancy Jean's arrival on May 5, 1965. As before with Jackie and Stevie, I refused to let mother and baby have the limelight and passed out cold when they were wheeled out by the nurses. In fact, I seemed to be getting worse rather than better, because this time I was out fifteen minutes, so worrying Barb's doctor, Bill Copeland, that he insisted on following us home to make sure we arrived safely. I was somewhat insulted by that, but finally had to suffer the indignity when he pointed out that I'd spent more time in the recovery room than my wife had. Here are the five of us, gathered next to the breakfast table at our then home in Columbus.

... And Outgunned

I won the old four-man format World Series of Golf four times in all, but not on this occasion, in 1965. Gary really did "stick me up" with a fine 139 for the two rounds. The other qualifiers that year, seen here on the left and right, respectively, were the Australian Peter Thomson, who had won his fifth British Open a few weeks previously, and our new PGA champion, Dave Marr. Thomson seemed to prefer faster course conditions than those common in the United States and so chose to play most of his golf under them. I've always rated Dave as the fellow who capitalized best on one big win, turning his Texas wit and attractive personality to great advantage in the commercial and television fields.

Good as the old World Series was to me, I always felt it was more a "television event" than a meaningful golf contest, so I was happy with the change to the present enlarged format. Now that the tournament is really getting close to wrapping up the season, and as long as the field contains strong international representation, I see no reason why it can't one day grow into the major event that the Tournament Players Division (TPD) is so eager to see it become.

Exit Time

We've always had the kids with us as much as possible at golf tournaments, and I've usually been the one to move them on or out when things got too boisterous. Here goes Jackie, aged five, at the PGA Championship in 1966.

No Help from Hoag

As I mentioned earlier, the Crosby is the one tournament apart from the majors that, through 1978, I have never missed since turning professional.

The only time in all those years I've been forced to lay up at the sixteenth at Cypress Point was here in the second round in 1967. One hole prior to this, I was leading the individual by about six shots, and my amateur partner, Bob Hoag, and I were also leading the pro-am team event. I then proceeded to finish the round double-bogey, double-bogey, double-bogey, par. Here's the middle double-bogey. I badly underestimated the strength of the wind and, attempting to lay up, hit a one-iron into the ocean.

Remarkably enough, I also started the third round with a double-bogey—four in five holes—and still won the individual tournament, which is an indication of just how tough conditions can be around Monterey Bay in January.

The team event, I'm sorry to say, escaped us. I'd put my life in dear old Bob Hoag's hands off a golf course, but the best thing about him in all the many Crosbys

we've now played together has definitely been his company. Here's the team's best-ball scoring during my little four-hole dose of the hacks: double-bogey, bogey, double-bogey, par. Naturally, we missed the cut. Nothing ever deflates Hoagy, though. Around Columbus he still tells everyone, "If Nicklaus would ever get his game in shape, we'd cakewalk the Crosby team event."

That's Hoagy in the dark sweater watching me try for a birdie at the seventh green at Pebble Beach, when he was still slim. I think this little 120-yard par 3 is one of the greatest holes in golf, ranging as it does from a flip wedge to a full five- or six-iron depending on wind conditions. Nearby us, of course, is the factor that makes the hole so scary even with a wedge in your hand—the Pacific Ocean.

Just Concentration, Folks

Here's the sort of expression that I'm told contributed to my cool reception by some of the fans back in my less trim days. Actually, it was then— and as the more recent picture shows, still is now—just the way my face happens to set when I am concentrating hard. In the first photo, I was on my way to tying the Olympia Fields course record with a 65, including only six one-putt greens, which set up the first of two consecutive wins in the Western Open. The year was 1967.

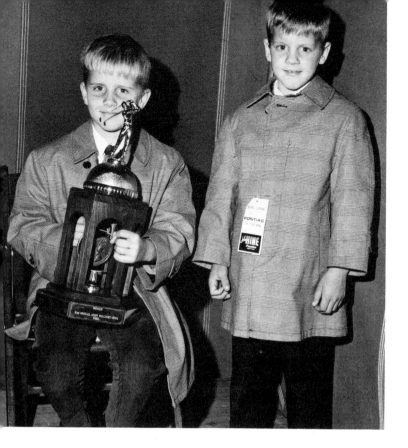

Only the Rag

Jackie and Stevie were along to watch me win the Andy Williams–San Diego Open in 1969. Seeing Jackie holding the trophy and Steve empty-handed here reminds me of their sister Nan's christening a few years earlier. Mainly to keep them quiet and attentive, the minister gave Jackie the bowl to hold and Steve the towel. After the ceremony, Barbara's father asked Steve if he'd enjoyed helping out. "Nope," he said. "I only got to hold the rag. Jackie got to hold the trophy." As I guess it is with most second children, that sort of thing has been the source of quite a few wrestling matches over the years, but I'm sure the fellows really do love each other, in the strange way brothers generally do.

You Think That's Funny?

Artists had a lot of fun with me after I lost weight. I didn't always see the funny side, but I thought this effort was pretty cute.

Partners

Hard as we've always tried to beat each other when playing for ourselves, Arnold and I have actually produced some of our finest golf when teamed together. Here's one of the seven wins we've enjoyed as a twosome, the National Four-Ball Championship in 1970 at the Laurel Valley Country Club, Arnie's "backyard."

We'd won in 1966 on my "home" turf, at the then PGA National in Florida, and we made it three in 1971 at Laurel Valley. The other four successes together were in the World Cup team championships in Paris in 1963, Hawaii in 1964, Tokyo in 1966, and Mexico City in 1967.

With us here, of course, are wives Winnie and Barbara.

107

A British Obstacle

Wentworth, England, 1970. I think it was Arnold who once said that if he had ever played three months straight off in British weather conditions, it would have taken him another three to get his swing back in shape. Following the sun as they generally do undoubtedly gives American pros a big advantage, because it is extremely difficult either to build a repeating swing or to sustain one in heavy winds and low temperatures.

The picture here shows another factor that I believe has to have an adverse bearing on British pro standards. That mini-jungle I'm beating out of is only a few yards off the fairway on one of the long par-4 holes at Wentworth, and penalizing rough of this kind close up to the mown area is pretty typical of many British courses. Leaving it that way certainly keeps maintenance costs and thus club dues down, but it also has an inhibiting affect on many good players, especially when courses become so dry—as they

108

often do in Britain—that even good shots will bounce and roll into this sort of trouble. The result is a tendency to "steer" the ball: to play defensively instead of aggressively, as we normally can in the States, with our cleared undergrowth in the roughs and our well-watered turf. In my view, that's why, with notable exceptions, the British pros aren't either as long or as bold as U.S. tour players.

I played in the Piccadilly a number of times, losing in the final to Gary Player in 1966 and winning on this occasion from Lee Trevino. It was an extremely well-run tournament from the players' point of view, although tough duty with thirty-six holes of head-to-head match play every day. Don't let the free-roaming gallery in the shot of Gary and me fool you—like all English fans, they were very well-behaved.

A Longtime Supporter

Mom has always liked to gallery, especially at home-state tournaments, where we can get together with family and friends after play. Here we are on the way to the first tee at the 1971 World Series. I finished second, one shot back of Masters champion Charlie Coody. With us here, in the "shades," is a member of my business team, Tom Peterson.

My Best-Ever Stretch

This brings back happy memories—the beginning of perhaps the finest stretch of golf I've ever played in my life, toward the end of 1971. It began here with a course-record 65 on the Royal Hobart course on the way to winning my third Australian Open by eight shots with a 269. The following week, playing the third round of the Australian Dunlop tournament, I drove to the fringe of the par-4 seventeenth and needed to get down in two and birdie the last hole to shoot a 59. I took three to get in the hole on seventeen and bogeyed the last hole for a 62, but went on to win again, by eight shots. The week after that, winning the World Cup at the then PGA National East Course with Lee Trevino, I shot a 271 to also take the individual title, this time by seven shots. It had been a poor year for me in the majors, with only the PGA Championship, but this little late-year burst sure helped to ease the pain.

to get more tired signing autographs than mine does. Going to write a book, I hear.

Seriously, Angelo has been an important part of my golf career almost as long as I've played the game professionally. We first got together in Palm Springs back in 1963, where I had gone to practice after missing my first cut on the tour in San Francisco. I had developed bursitis in my hip, which made walking painful, and was playing a few holes at Indian Wells using a golf cart, when the caddie master came out and told me he had the caddie who had been "assigned" to me for the upcoming Palm Springs Classic. That irritated me a little bit, because both the tour custom and my preference is to choose a caddie rather than have one arbitrarily selected for me. However, I didn't have anyone in mind for the week, so I told the

A Degree At Last

Despite not finishing my formal education at Ohio State, I did eventually get an honorary degree, as a Doctor of Athletic Arts. Jesse Owens received a similar degree at the same ceremony in 1972, and I believe we're the only two alumni to be so honored by the school.

Even though I believe it was partly an apology for not letting me finish my studies in my own time, I enjoyed the occasion and appreciated the gesture.

Angelo Argea

Here he is, the world's most famous caddie! That hand he's waving is beginning

caddie master to send the fellow on out and I'd see how we got along.

The fellow proved to be Angelo. We got along fine right away, and by the end of the week we had won the tournament. So three months later, I asked him to caddie for me at the Tournament of Champions, and we won there too. The following year in Palm Springs did not produce a win, but a few days later we won together in Phoenix and went on to repeat in the Tournament of Champions and the Sahara later in the year. By then, of course, Angelo was becoming sort of "my boy" (or me his boy—I've never been sure which), especially in Western events, and over the next three or four years he gradually became full-time with me.

What I basically seek in a caddie is promptness, alertness and quietness. Angie's always met the last two criteria and almost always the first. He did slip a few years ago by not showing up three times in a week, but the three months off it cost him seems to have permanently made the point about dependability.

Like a lot of caddies, there was a time when Angie had a fire in his pocket that just wouldn't go out—he'd go to Las Vegas for a week and could never afford to leave! We began to ease that problem a few years back by putting him on a regular salary administered by my business office, and I think now life has taken on a whole new complexion for him. In fact, just recently he bought a condominium, which is the first thing of substance he's ever owned. Next thing, I guess, he'll be getting married—which will definitely break a few hearts around the world!

112

Jimmy Dickinson

There's a definite "star" system among British tour caddies, just as there is here in the United States, and obviously the top men go for the prominent Americans in the British Open because they are usually among the favorites. Before I went over for the British Open in 1963, someone told me that Jimmy Dickinson was an excellent caddie and a fine man, so I hired him, and that's how it has proved to be ever since. Here we are at Muirfield in Scotland in 1972.

Jimmy is a Yorkshireman and has worked mainly at Wentworth near London between tour engagements. Because of the insecurity of the life, I offered him a position at Muirfield Village when we opened the club in 1973, and he did a nice job for us. But both he and his wife found it difficult to adjust to the American scene and decided to go home after a couple of years. Injuries prevented Jimmy from caddying for me in the 1976 and 1977 British Opens, but he was with me again for the

1977 Ryder Cup matches and, I hope, will be for future British Opens.

Jimmy's a super caddie and a very good fellow, but he has one problem, which is me! Apparently, I make him terribly nervous, to the point where anytime he knows I'm coming his stomach starts to hurt! A lot of people, including me, have told him my bark is much worse than my bite, but it doesn't seem to stop Jimmy from growing ulcers working for me.

The Fans

These scenes at the 1972 PGA Championship and 1977 Masters are fairly typical of most tournaments. Once I've finished playing, I never mind signing autographs, as long as I can do it without people climbing all over me. My biggest fear in the kind of crush you see in the first photo is getting jabbed in the eye with a pen or pencil. I've been poked in the face at least fifteen times over the years, and I guess have just been lucky that it wasn't in the wrong spot. If the people are orderly, I'll stand around for an hour or more and try to make everyone happy. If they're using me as a basketball, I'm usually in the clubhouse within five minutes. As it does with just about everything, the Masters handles this situation very well (second photo) by running you in a golf cart from the eighteenth green to the press facility or the locker room.

Basically, I enjoy the fans a lot. Obviously it's flattering to be the subject of

so much attention, but it goes deeper than that. These are the people who pay the piper. If they weren't there, neither would I be. As public entertainers, which is what professional tournament golfers essentially are, I feel we owe the fans a part of our day as a direct personal return for their support. There are twenty-four hours in a day, so if you give the fans just a little time after your round, you are not really sacrificing an awful lot of your life. I just try to hold the time until after I've played—and to come out without too many scars.

Match Play

Most pros don't like match play, and there are three reasons why. One is the risk of getting beaten by an inferior golfer running hot for a few hours. Another is the uncertainty as to the paycheck. The third is the psychological impact of actually being beaten and eliminated, as opposed to finishing down the field but not really "losing" (as you can kid yourself happens in stroke play).

I understand those sentiments and all the other negatives, such as the problems of television coverage, but I still think it is a shame that we don't have at least one match-play tour event in the States, because such tournaments really are more fun to watch than all but the last few holes of most stroke-play events.

Here's the man behind the only match-play tournament held during my time on tour, Milt Harrington, then president of

Liggett & Myers. As did Joe Dey, the TPD commissioner at the time, Milt had a lot of courage in backing the U.S. Professional Match-Play Championship at such an out-of-the-way spot as Pinehurst. Unfortunately, for all the reasons I've just indicated, the event survived only three years (1971–73), but I was proud to have added it to my record in 1972 with a 2 and 1 win over Frank Beard at the Country Club of North Carolina. Apart from Ryder Cup matches, the only other match-play contest I have won as a professional is the Piccadilly World Match Play at Wentworth in England in 1970 (now sponsored by Colgate).

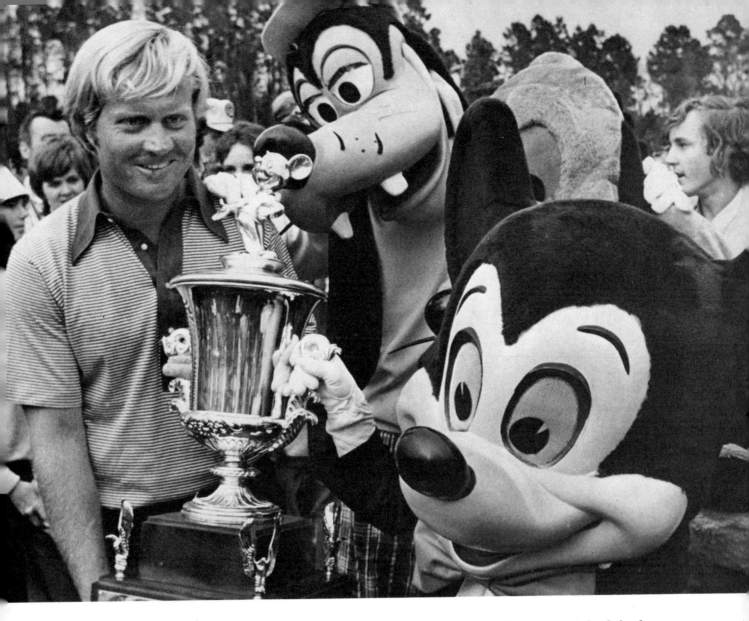

Batting 1,000

Here's the one tournament I've won every year it was played, 1971 through 1973—the Disney World Open. (Maybe that's why the people at Disney World changed the format to a team championship after 1973!)

The picture with Goofy and Mickey shows the conclusion of the 1972 event, and my twenty-one-under-par score of 267 reflected the very fine year I had had. Bobby Mitchell finished second, nine shots back.

Like many of the pros, when I wasn't on the course during the Disney tournaments, I was generally in the Magic Kingdom—I've been in and on everything there probably twenty times, and I still love it all as much as the first time. Great ice cream too. Just a big overgrown kid, I guess.

I Think I'll Keep Going at It Right-Handed

When forced to, I've occasionally played left-handed recovery shots in tournaments with the blade of an iron club inverted, but I hadn't tried an actual left-handed club in a long time when this picture was taken in 1973. The event was the Esquire Magazine Invitational in Miami, and I just suddenly had the urge to try a shot with one of my partner's left-handed clubs. I hit a neat little blooper into the lake right in front of me.

My One 59

I've never really come close to doing a "Geiberger"—shooting a 59 during a regular tour event. My tournament low is 62, achieved three times between 1967 and 1973. But as the card shows, I did manage to break 60 during an exhibition in 1973 at the Breakers Hotel course in Palm Beach. It's a short layout with a number of drivable par 4s, but it has some tricky features, and I felt the score represented pretty good golf. The other scores that day would seem to indicate that: Sam Snead and Kathy Whitworth shot 69 and Kathy Ahern 74.

9 · Birdies – 1 Eagle – 8 · Pars --   11 - 3's
1 - 2
8 - Pars
No Bogies

Official Record — Course Holder
All putts holed.

Hole	Men's Course	Men's Par	Sam Snead	Kathy Whitworth	Handicap	Strokes (Nicklaus)	Kathy Ahern	+/- 0	Ladies' Course	Ladies' Par
1	348	4	3	4	11	(3)	4	—	348	4
2	356	4	4	4	7	(3)	4	+1	356	4
3	350	4	4	4	9	4	4	+1	330	4
4	125	3	2	3	17	(2)	3	+1	125	3
5	370	4	4	4	5	(3)	5	+2	338	4
6	398	4	4	4	1	4	4	+2	362	5
7	297	4	4	4	13	(3)	4	+3	297	4
8	301	4	3	3	15	(3)	4	+3	301	4
9	379	4	4	3	3	4	4	+1	379	4
Out	2924	35	32	33		29	36		2836	36
10	200	3	3	3	18	3	3	+2	152	3
11	370	4	4	4	8	(3)	4	+3	324	4
12	460	5	4	4	4	(3)	4	+4	420	5
13	225	3	4	4	14	3	3	+4	204	3
14	431	4	4	4	2	4	4	+5	390	5
15	353	4	4	4	12	(3)	4	+6	353	4
16	349	4	4	4	10	4	5	+6	349	4
17	349	4	4	4	6	4	4	+6	349	4
18	347	4	4	4	16	(3)	3	+7	347	4
In	3084	35	37	36		30	38		2888	36
Tot.	6008	70	69	69		(59)	74		5724	72
Handicap										
Net Score				All Time Course Record						

PLAYER _Jack Nicklaus_

ATTEST _Kelvin Holden_ DATE _Mar-12-73_
(Chairman)

117

A Better One-Iron

This had to be in as a contrast to the picture on page 103!

What I'm doing here is marking my tee shot at the sixteenth at Cypress Point in the 1973 Crosby—after another one-iron shot on another cold and windy day. The birdie that followed was the first I'd ever made on the hole in more than thirty rounds of Crosby practice and tournament play, and through 1977 I've made only one more since. Despite triple-bogeying the very next hole, I managed to defend my title by winning a play-off with Orville Moody and Ray Floyd. That's Bob Hoag in the background, by the way—calling for another ball by the looks of it!

The Club Master

A lot of tour pros get very scientific about their clubs, Arnold Palmer being the game's best-known "fiddler," of course. Arnie has an engineering plant at his home that most club manufacturers would be proud of, and I believe he still spends a lot of time in it simply because he enjoys the work so much.

I've become more conscious of the technological side of equipment as I've become more involved in recent years in working on the design of MacGregor clubs. But here's the real club master, the fellow in the glasses, David Graham. David really has studied the science (or is it art?) of club design, both for his own

118

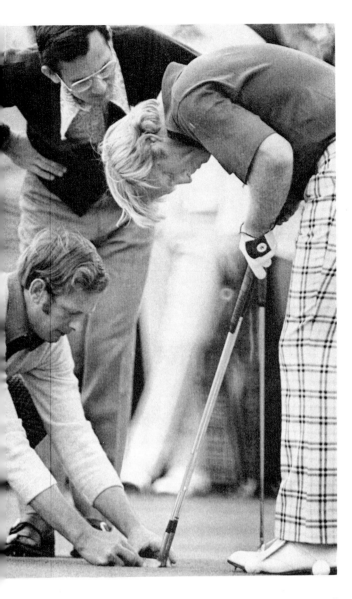

benefit as a player and with the hope of making a career in equipment manufacturing when his tour days are over. Here we are at the 1973 Masters, checking out a copy of my putter that David had made for me to use as a spare. Dave's fellow Aussie, Bruce Devlin, is giving the work a critical once-over.

Number Five

Here's our youngest, Michael Scott, born July 24, 1973. Despite his youth—five months when this picture was taken—there were signs of at least one sporting interest: mountaineering. All the kids have been pretty agile, but Mike soon became the champion climber—of anything and everything, including the kitchen cabinets.

119

The Ryder Cup

This was a fun practice foursome at Muirfield in Scotland in 1973—the other players are Billy Casper, Arnold Palmer and Lee Trevino, with the U.S. team captain, Jack Burke, Jr., standing next to Lee on his right.

I've played in all five Ryder Cup matches since I became eligible for the U.S. team in 1969, and I have greatly enjoyed both the camaraderie of the event and the relationships and goodwill that it promotes. However, I also happen to feel that as a golf contest pure and simple, it badly needs a change in format.* As far as

* A change was made as we went to press, creating in effect a Europe vs. U.S.A. format for future matches.

the American players are concerned, everyone wants and enjoys the honor of making the team, but many find it difficult to get charged up for the matches themselves. By saying this, I'm not trying to put down my British friends, but the fact has to be faced that British professional golf in recent years simply hasn't developed a sufficient depth of good players to make a true contest out of the event. Nor, from what I see, does there appear to be much likelihood of that situation changing in the foreseeable future.

I know national pride is involved here, but at some point reality must prevail if the event isn't to decline into little more than an exhibition bout—and especially if it is to remain a vital part of the U.S. golfing calendar. If from the players' standpoint the event could be regarded simply as an expression of international goodwill rather than as a real contest, then certainly the present format would suit all the participants. Unfortunately, that is impossible in terms of both public and press reaction to the outcome—especially in Britain, where the match gets much more exposure and stirs much greater emotions than it does in the United States.

When you consider that the golfing population of the United States is roughly equivalent to that of the rest of the world, maybe a World versus the United States format would make the most sense (it would certainly present the American players with the toughest possible challenge). If that's too presumptuous, then the United States versus the English-speaking Countries or even the United States versus Europe would seem viable formats. What I would like to see is the PGAs of both countries getting together and facing this problem squarely before it gets so out of hand that the spirit of the event is destroyed.

Muirfield Village

The thought of building my own golf course and club in my own hometown had been frequently in my mind for many years before I was in a position to give any sort of substance to such a vision. The main stimulus, once I became successful as a professional, was to try to give a little something—and something permanent— back to the game that had given me so much. Although in order to pursue my profession year round I live in Florida, my heart and my oldest friends and deepest associations have always been in Columbus, where I was born and grew up and went to school and got married. Columbus had had a very successful charity pro-am for years, which I did my best to support, but never an ongoing full-scale tournament, nor much top sport of any kind beyond Ohio State football and occasionally basketball. The prospect of one day helping to fill that gap with an annual golf event run comparably to major-championship standards added more excitement to the dream.

The dream has been a reality now for a number of years in the shape of Muirfield Village Golf Club and the Memorial Tour-

nament, and here are five of the people who most helped to make it come true. Ivor Young, on the far left, a longtime friend from Scioto, was the fellow who found the marvelous piece of land we were able to acquire and who directed the business side of its acquisition. Pro Jim Gerring, next to him, has built and run the golf operation from day one—to a point where even I have to struggle to find flaws—and has won the universal respect and friendship of an international membership. Pandel Savic and Bob Hoag, to the left and right of me, respectively, also old friends from early Scioto days, gave so

much effort to getting the club off the ground that it seemed at one stage as though they had virtually given up their own businesses, and they continue to carry a hefty load as Memorial Tournament co-chairmen. Ed Etchells, on the far right, who began by directing the construction of the course, is our superintendent—and, as far as I am concerned, the finest in the country.

This picture was taken on the eighteenth green in the fall of 1974. We had opened the course four months previously, on Memorial Day, 1974.

122

Here's a shot from earlier that day. I've never been too good at waiting around for other people to do things that I feel are important, especially where the Memorial Course is concerned.

Major-Championship "Insurance"

So far I don't regard myself as having won major championships in 1974 and 1976, but here's my insurance.

Ever since the birth of the Tournament Players Championship in 1974, there has been a strong effort by Commissioner Deane Beman and his troops to build the image of the tournament to major-championship status. Having won the event in 1974 and again in 1976, I figure that if this effort succeeds I'm in good shape, not only for those two otherwise majorless years, but also for my overall total!

Seriously, I think the concept of a players' championship is excellent, and the event immediately became and will remain one of the most significant tournaments on the U.S. tour. As for its becoming a true major in the eyes of the rest of the world, I fear the event simply doesn't have enough overseas representation under its present qualification format to ring many bells outside North America. I think the new World Series of Golf has a much better chance in that respect—which is another reason I'm glad to have won *its* inaugural in 1976. Who knows? Maybe in a few years I'll be able to add three more championships to the tally without even drawing back a club!

One of my favorite pictures (page 124, top) shows two of my oldest friends in golf, Joe Dey (left) and Deane Beman. I met both of them for the first time at the first USGA event I played in, the 1953 National Junior, when I was thirteen. Joe was then the USGA's executive director, and Deane was the medalist that year. Following his distinguished career at the USGA, Joe became our first commissioner when the PGA and the players agreed to put the tour under the control of a Tournament Players Division, then handed the reins over to Deane when he retired. Both have done great work for the game, and both have contributed very heavily to my career with their firm friendship and good counsel on all sorts of matters, golfing and otherwise.

The TPC trophy here was named for Joe in recognition of his contribution to professional tournament golf, and I'm very proud to possess an award with his name on it.

The "Hawaiian Elephant"

Yes, it is a very big check in every respect, but that's not how it came by its nickname.

I happen to be a great lover of animal art, and in 1974 Barbara and I decided to have an elephant scene painted by David Shepherd, the eminent English artist, who specializes in wildlife art. I'd mentioned this around the office, and some of my business associates—protecting my interests, of course, so they thought—felt that it would be a considerable extravagance at that particular moment. I hadn't intended to play in the Hawaiian Open that year, but we wanted the painting, so I said, "To heck with you guys, I'm going to go *win* what it takes to get it."

Fortunately, my game that week was as big as my mouth—hence the "Hawaiian Elephant."

Tough Challenge

Here's old friend Jack Grout facing one of his sterner challenges—teaching Barbara at Augusta National in 1974 for an article *Golf Digest* was doing on his methods. Barb did quite well at golf as a beginner in college, but playing the game has never really turned her on. She's much fonder of tennis—and much better at it, I might add.

Seeing Jack here with Mrs. Nicklaus reminds me of how he got hitched way back in the days when he was still playing the winter tour (he's played with every great golfer of this century except Harry Vardon). Seems he had nothing much to do one evening, so a pal fixed him up with a blind date. The girl's name was Bonnie, and Jack liked her so much that, after dinner and a drive, he proposed to her that very evening. I don't know what the statistics show about the longevity of liaisons made like that, but I do know I've never met a happier couple than they are.

An Added Challenge

Here's one of the additional golfing challenges you face in Japan: converting meters into yards. I was playing an exhibition match against Jumbo Osaki in Tokyo in 1974 at a course I hadn't seen before. You need help in situations like that, and providing it here are a member of my management team, Bill Sansing, and a good friend of ours, Kumboh Yanagawa, the president of a large Japanese optical company. Bill was the fellow who finally stopped me from looking like a refugee from an army and navy store by initiating my association with Hart Schaffner & Marx back in the mid-sixties. I had no apparel-endorsement arrangement at that time and happened to mention the fact one day to Bob Hope, who had had a long and happy association with Hart. Typical of Bob, he called Hart, where Bill was then running sales and marketing, and the then president of the company, Jim Wilson, Bill and myself met at the Western Open that year. The association started out modestly but has grown to be very significant for both parties over the years, in Japan as well as in the United States.

125

Teaching Children

Gary Thomas, our fourth child, had arrived January 15, 1969. Here he is in 1975, aged six, on the practice tee at Lost Tree, showing excellent form for his years. In fact, there's very little you could fault about this action considering his strength at the time: basically all the moves are excellent, particularly the way he's stayed down and back through the ball.

As with the other children, Gary has learned his golf chiefly by imitation—he's always enjoyed coming over to the practice tee and the golf course with me and mimicking what he saw me doing. When I've noticed something way out of line, I've pointed it out to him as simply as possible, but I've never really given him lessons in the formal sense.

I think this is the ideal way for most kids to start golf, especially if they have the opportunity to watch and be around good players. Children are great copiers and, if they enjoy beating balls around, will generally develop at least the rudiments of a good swinging motion just by observation. Once they've gotten that, adjusting and fine tuning the action as they get older and stronger becomes comparatively simple. Without a good innate swinging motion, of course, they are always going to struggle at the game. Therefore, I have made a deliberate effort with all my kids never to impose anything on them in the way of technique that might have an inhibiting effect on their natural tendency simply to swing the club through the ball as freely as possible.

126

127

Letting children learn by imitation doesn't mean, of course, that they will always be interested in *your* game. Here's Gary, a little later the same year, "watching" me coming down to the wire in the Doral Eastern Open!

A Misapprehension

A lot of people in golf love to fish, including many of the tour players, but I don't know of anyone with more enthusiasm than this guy, bouncing around with me here somewhere out along the Great Barrier Reef. He's John Montgomery, and you can generally find him in only three places: out on a boat, out in some remote wilderness with a gun under his arm, or at one of the twenty or so pro tournaments he currently runs in North America, Japan and Australia. John has been a very close friend of our family for years, but much as Barbara loves him, she gets very nervous anytime he calls because the chances are odds on that he's going to try to entice me

on some fishing or hunting expedition. To him, these activities aren't hobbies or sports: they are *passions*. Get him and Tom Weiskopf together and your ears will fall off before they get done talking water and wilderness.

John and I first discovered our mutual love of fishing about eight years ago, when he came to me for help in setting up his tournament-organizing company, Executive Sports, Inc. My own company, Golden Bear, Inc., initially took a minority stock position in that operation in return for partial funding assistance. My indirect involvement eventually led to some concern among a few tour players, who felt that I had a voice and a business interest in the conduct of the tour. At that time, in 1973, I divested myself of all interest in Executive Sports. Unfortunately, a lot of people in pro golf still seem to be under the misapprehension that I'm somehow involved in running part of the tour—probably because John and I remain such close friends. For the record, it simply isn't so.

A Prized Award

The world has been very generous to me over the years with awards and honors. I'm proud to have all of them, but here's one that is especially dear—the PGA Player of the Year Award. Then PGA president Henry Poe is making this presentation in 1975. I've also been given the award in four other years by the PGA, and a similar one twice by the golf writers of America.

Is This Picture Flipped?

No, the glove is on the left hand and the club is upside down, so I was actually swinging left-handed. The shot worked too—well enough for me to par the hole and go on to win the tournament: Heritage Classic, Sea Pines Plantation, Hilton Head Island, 1975.

Hey, Good-Looking!

I'm biased, of course, but I really do think Barbara has gotten prettier as she's gotten older. This is one of my favorite pictures of her, taken during the 1976 Tournament Players Championship at Inverrary (which I happened to win). Shows the right sort of spectating commitment too!

A Memento for the President

President Ford was in Columbus campaigning for reelection during our first

Memorial Tournament in 1976, but his schedule wouldn't permit a visit to the course. As he was our honorary chairman, we wanted him to at least have a memento of the event. When I suggested to him that Barbara drop it off, he said, "I'd love her to." Here she is doing just that. I'm not sure she expected quite the ceremony that transpired, but she handled it beautifully, as she does all public occasions, despite her shyness about being in the limelight.

The memento we chose was our main pro-am gift, an exact copy of Bobby Jones's putter, "Calamity Jane." Jones was our honoree that first year, and the reproduction of his famous club was so popular that we've continued the idea, giving a copy of Walter Hagen's mid-mashie in 1977 and of Francis Ouimet's jigger in 1978.

Looking on here are two good friends of both of us, Ohio State football coach Woody Hayes and the governor of Ohio on and off for many years, Jim Rhodes. Woody gets some hot press at times, but I've always felt his integrity and the standards he sets and adheres to more than offset his occasional temper flare-ups. As for Jim, as governor he has probably done more for the people of Ohio than any other public official. He's also a heck of a good golfer, about a three- or four-handicapper.

Nicklaus & Nicklaus

I don't know when we'll do business next, but this really was a great firm—my eldest son, Jack, caddying for me in the 1976 British Open at Royal Birkdale. Jimmy Dickinson, my regular British caddie, had injured an Achilles tendon the day before the tournament started. Jack was along on vacation, so I said to him, "Come on, let's go," and he jumped at the chance. Although he had never really caddied before—certainly not in a big tournament—he did a fabulous job, absolutely on the button from start to finish. In fact, it was the only time I can remember that I've never had a caddie tell me what to do, never had a wrong club in my hand, never had a disagreement about a shot. Obviously, Jack's own golf knowledge helped a lot—he was shooting mostly under 80 at this time.

I might just add that having a job to do didn't spoil his own fun, either. Despite his footsoreness and the tropical heat that week, he played golf just about every day as soon as he was through with my game. Oh, for the energy of youth!

What's That Guy Doing?

Less experienced fans often look a little puzzled when I go through this sort of maneuver on the golf course. It's part of my loosening-up ritual on the practice tee or anytime I've had to wait a while between shots. The exercise you see here (the tournament is the 1976 PGA Championship at Congressional in Washington) is to stretch my lower back, and I do a couple of others to limber up my upper back and shoulders and my arms and wrists. I also do about ten minutes of exercises in the room every day when I'm playing golf, and I always warm up slowly on the practice range by building from the shorter clubs up to the woods. I've had a few minor back problems all my life, chiefly related to muscle tension, but they certainly weren't what put me two behind Dave Stockton in defending this particular championship: a balky putter had a lot more to do with that generally frustrating week.

Golf Course Designing

At least half the traveling I've done in recent years has been in connection with designing golf courses. Here's the farthest I've ever been on such an assignment and also the most unlikely design "office" I've yet used. The place is the Great Barrier Reef off the northeastern coast of Australia, and the "office" is the cabin of our mother ship, the *Tropic Queen*.

What we were working on so assiduously here, back in the fall of 1976, were concepts for the redesign of the Australian Golf Club course in Sydney, now the permanent site of the Australian Open. I had told Kerry Packer, the sponsor of the event (looking over my shoulder here), that the course could stand some improvement when I played over there in 1975, and he had invited me to submit ideas. Kerry loves the outdoors as much as I do, so we decided to combine business with pleasure and work on the plans during a week's fishing off the reef prior to the 1976 Australian Open. Arbitrating here—Kerry is a man of strong opinions—are, from left to right, the president of Golden Bear, Inc., Chuck Perry; longtime friend and fishing companion John Montgomery, who runs the Australian Open, along with numerous U.S. and Japanese tour events; and a friend of Kerry's, Alan Sawyer. The fellow down in the right-hand corner, hiding behind the cigar, is my Columbus pal Pandel Savic. By the end of the week, Kerry had accepted all the plans, and we began work shortly thereafter. We had so much fun that we made some more plans: for an-

other fishing expedition, in New Zealand this time, the week before the 1977 Australian Open.

I became interested in course design right from the moment I began to travel extensively to play the game, first through analyzing the playing characteristics of holes and then from a purely aesthetic perspective. The creative challenge of the work appealed to me, but what really got me active in the business were all the poorly designed courses I ran across as I traveled around the world to play golf. Maybe we just built courses too fast and with too little forethought during golf's big boom years, but whatever the reasons, we sure created an awful lot of dogs, in terms of both playability and the use of land. I'd seen many of the truly great golf courses in the world—most of them built before World War II, incidentally—and increasingly I wanted to use that experi-

ence to make my own tangible and permanent statement about the game. I first began to dabble at the job back in the late sixties, but have escalated it into a second career in recent years, with a full-time sales and design organization based at my North Palm Beach offices. I see it as an ideal way of staying in and around golf once I finish competing.

Had I been able to anticipate this direction in my school years, I'm certain I would have taken college courses in the disciplines involved. As it is, I've learned as I've gone along, as I have in business management. Naturally, I've made mistakes—show me a golf course designer who hasn't. But I'm a pretty quick study, and I don't think they'll be repeated, especially in the area of using existing land to its best advantage and in making a course a *fun* place to be as well as a challenging test of the game.

133

Big Doings Down Under

Having won it five times, I'm particularly fond of the Australian Open—in fact, of Australia and Australians generally. This picture is from the pro-am prior to the last of those wins, in 1976.

We introduced the fellow on my left, Kerry Packer, in the previous picture, but if you know anything about cricket you have probably heard of him before: he's the fellow who in 1977 set the cricketing world on its head by signing up just about all the top professionals for a new world tour designed to provide programming for his television stations. Cricket is probably the number-one spectator sport in Australia, and when Kerry couldn't get the TV rights to the top international games through the traditional channels, he simply went ahead and virtually bought up the pro game lock, stock and barrel. The wherewithal, such as the large sums he's invested in upgrading the Australian

Open in the past few years, comes from the publishing/TV conglomerate he inherited from his father, the late Sir Frank Packer, a famous figure in Americas Cup yacht racing as well as a major name in Australian business. Also with us here are our other golfing partners that day, my pal Pandel Savic (in the hat) and that unique man of tennis, Bobby Riggs, just teeing off.

If Packer has his way—and he usually does—I think there is a very good chance that the Australian Open will eventually come to be regarded as a major event in world golf. As I just mentioned, Kerry hired me to redesign the Australian Golf Club course in Sydney as a permanent home for the championship, and he has been very successful in getting hole-by-hole sponsorship from top companies of the type you see reflected here. He has also made the tournament unique in the world of golf by televising the entire four days of play from start to finish. The result

134

has been an increase in prize money to top U.S. standards since 1976, which is beginning to bring in the best players from all over the world—the primary factor in building a major.

"Air Bear"

Both Barbara and I, having always been taught the value of a dollar, were highly budget-conscious when we first started traveling the tour, so we began by driving from tournament to tournament, particularly in the West. This worked reasonably well with one youngster, Jackie; but when Stevie arrived in April 1963, it got to be a pain in the neck, so we decided to fly between most of the tour stops—commercially, of course, and usually in the back of the bus. By 1964, however, I had gotten myself into so many different activities that, after much soul-searching, we decided to get a private plane. Thus began the saga of what has come to be known among my friends and colleagues as "Air Bear."

The first plane in the Air Bear fleet was an Aero Commander 680 FL, a fat-bellied, high-winged, twin-engined prop job. Over the next four years, in addition to a course of single-engine lessons, my pilot, Stanley Pierce, who was also an instructor, put me

through at least eight-hundred hours in this airplane, and I thoroughly enjoyed every one of them.

The Aero Commander was a fine plane, with a cruising speed of about 220 mph and a range of a thousand miles, but by 1967 my schedule had become even more complex. Determined to get home to my growing family as much as possible, I began to hanker for something faster. So we leased a Learjet 24, a very neat little plane, with a top speed of 550 mph and a range of fifteen hundred miles. As before, Stan Pierce continued to be chief pilot, but at that time I decided I had better get serious about flying or give it up entirely and leave it to the pros. After a little more instruction, I decided on the latter course and have never regretted it.

In 1968, we leased a Lear 25. Air Bear continued with the Lear 25 for two years, but in 1970, with costs getting out of hand, we closed it down for a year, reopening in 1972 by chartering small jets as needed. That continued for the better part of five years, but costs again began to make nasty dents in the ledgers (we were logging up to four hundred hours of flying time a year), so in late 1976 we decided to lease another plane and make it available for charter when not in Air Bear service. Here it is, a Cessna Citation, on delivery day at Monterey during the 1977 Crosby.

Funny how life sometimes goes in a cir-

cle. The gentleman handing me the keys is Russ Meyer, chairman of Cessna. Russ, an attorney, set up my Aero Commander deal when he was putting together golf exhibitions for Mark McCormack back in 1964. He later went into the aviation business, eventually rising to the top job at Cessna. "Well, here we are, going around again," was our mutual greeting when I called to talk about the Citation.

One final comment on Air Bear. I know people often think a private plane is more a personal luxury than a business tool, but that is simply not so in my case. Every single one of my professional activities requires constant travel, usually long distance, and I would be three times less productive without this tool, as would my top company executives.

Japan

Here's an unusual experience: dinner in a Buddhist temple in Toyko, hosted by my good friend Tak Kaneda and organized by a monk who directed some television shows I made in 1977. The monk's name is Yoshimune Sugawara, and as a former top TV golf director, he'd been persuaded by the packagers to take a leave of absence from the temple to work on my shows. He and a sixteen-man crew came over from Tokyo for the shooting at Frenchman's Creek near my home in Florida, and they did a marvelous job of making two forty-five-minute instructional programs based on my *Lesson Tee* book. The food here at Sugawara-san's temple, incidentally, was tempura, one of my favorites among the dozens of Japanese cuisines—washed down, for those who didn't care for sake, with water drawn from a five-hundred-year-old indoor well situated just behind where I'm sitting. Next to me is Mitsuo Hirose, an executive of Dai Nippon Printing Company, one of the organizations I work with in Japan, and next to "Mike," as we call him, is Chuck Perry, the president of my own company, Golden Bear, Inc.

I first went to Japan in 1963 for some exhibition games and then again in 1966 to play in the World Cup with Arnold Palmer (we won). In recent years, I've been there increasingly often, first to design the New St. Andrews course for Zenya Hamada (seen on page 137 with his wife, and Barbara in a lovely kimono they had just presented her) and latterly to service the many business associations we have developed over there. It's a fascinating country, and a unique golf scene has developed there since two home players, Torakichi Nakamura and Koichi Ono, first put the game on the map by winning the Canada Cup in Tokyo in 1957 from Sam Snead and Jimmy Demaret.

I'm sure most of the Japanese who take up golf fall genuinely in love with it, but there's no doubt that the initial impetus

for many is status, both business and social. Because of the shortage of land (the government now prohibits golf course construction on land that can be used for building or agriculture), club golf is incredibly expensive. The boom appeared to peak with the economic recession brought about by the 1973–1974 oil shortage; but at one time, bonds ran as high as $100,000 for membership at top-rate courses within reasonable reach of major cities (which, in Japan, means within a hundred miles). On top of that, there are usually annual dues, plus green fees every time you play the course, plus very high costs and taxes for all the ancillary equipment and services. Not surprisingly, most memberships are corporate rather than individual, a part of the management advancement perquisite system that is such a feature of Japan's business structure. If you don't fit into that framework, tough luck. There are very few public courses as we know them, and the best you can hope for—beyond beating balls into a driving range net—is an occasional game as someone's guest.

For top U.S. pros, of course, Japan can be a bonanza, in both income opportunities and hospitality. You need a strong stomach for the constant entertainment and a lot of patience for the long rides to and from courses through some of the world's worst traffic, but the enthusiasm and graciousness of the people are matchless. Unfortunately, with a few notable exceptions, the design of the courses isn't inspired; but with so much hand labor, their condition generally is excellent.

Most of my golf in Japan until now has been exhibitions, but I hope to play a tournament or two over there in the years ahead. One thing for sure is that the competition isn't getting any easier: with purses beginning to approach U.S. levels, Japanese pros have been getting better and better in recent years. In fact, they probably have more good tournament players today than any nation in the world after the United States—although the Spaniards have recently gotten pretty hot on their tails.

My Biggest Golfing Thrill

Just a couple of old folks still in love!

What we're celebrating so smoochily here is my single biggest thrill in golf. Ever since I began to make a name for myself in the game, I'd dreamed of one day winning in my hometown on a course I had designed and built myself and in a tournament I had had a hand in creating. The possibility of doing all that was so remote for so long that I never allowed it to become more than a very private fantasy. But on May 23, 1977, it all came true when I won the second Memorial Tournament at Muirfield Village by two strokes from Hubert Green. The emotion was so strong right after I'd tapped in the final putt that for a few moments I even thought about retiring from the game as a regular tournament player. Thankfully, Barbara's wise counsel prevented me from announcing such a decision, because it is one that I'm sure I would have regretted.

It was nice at this moment to have two of my oldest friends on hand, Bob Hoag (left) and Pandel Savic, to make the trophy presentation as co-chairmen of the tournament. Seeing Pandel here looking so fatherly reminds me of how we first ran into each other way back when I was wearing short pants. My dad's first drugstore was on the Ohio State campus, and Pandel would drop in occasionally on his way to school. I knew him because of his football record—he was an All Big Ten quarterback on OSU and led the team to a Rose Bowl victory in 1950—but we'd never met until he caught me in the store one day stuffing my pockets with candy. Honest as a solid drive, Pandel still regarded me suspiciously for quite a time even after my Aunt Nell, clerking that day, had convinced him I was the owner's son. A very down-to-earth fellow, he's continued to be my conscience on many other matters since that first meeting.

138

Chapter 5
Some Moments I'd Rather Have Missed

"Our Leader"

Including this picture comes under the heading of labor relations. My office staff insisted it be in the book.

The time is early 1962, and I'm now a pro. The bedroom slippers and pajama top show that I've just gotten out of bed. I'd recently signed a new slacks contract, and the first batch had just arrived in the mail (they were definitely not Hart Schaffner & Marx pants, let me quickly add). An advertising photo session was coming up, and this was the first attempt at fitting me.

For many years, my secretary, Linda Schweitzer, had a framed blowup of this picture prominently displayed on her office wall over the title "Our Leader." I snuck it out one night and burned it.

All Part of the Learning Process

Here's an example of how *not* to approach tournament golf. The event is the 1962 Piccadilly Tournament (the forerunner of the Piccadilly World Match Play) at Hillside Golf Club next door to Royal Birkdale in northwestern England. It was my first pro tournament overseas, and I don't think I could have made more mistakes if I'd actually tried to. Among the worst were giving myself only two days to get used to the course and the time change—and no prior practice with the smaller-size British ball. Coming from 90-degree weather in Texas to 40 degrees and 30-mph winds didn't help any, either. The

result was 298 for the seventy-two holes, considerable embarrassment and a lasting lesson.

With me here is playing partner Guy Wolstenholme, who had recently turned pro after a fine amateur career. The bobby doesn't look very busy, but at English golf events they rarely have to be because the galleries are so well-mannered.

Incidentally, my impression of the Hill-side golf course on that trip was that it was one of the worst I'd ever played. Fourteen years later, having a rather better understanding of British conditions, I walked around it with my son Jack one day during the British Open week and was amazed to find what a fine golf course it actually is. I guess not making snap judgments is another lesson that comes with age.

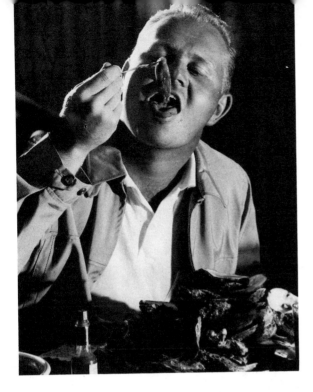

Final-Round Fix

As good a golfer as I was becoming in those early tour days, I was a still better eater! Here, I'm getting ready for the final round of the 1963 New Orleans Open with some oysters before dinner—eight dozen of them, as I recall. Can you imagine that? Eight dozen oysters *before dinner!* No wonder I finished nine shots behind Bo Wininger.

Someone Forget to Cut the Fairway?

British Open, Royal Birkdale, 1965. The opening hole here is a par 5, usually reachable in two, but here's what you find yourself in if you go about ten feet through the green. I believe in rough, but I think the British tend to overdo it sometimes.

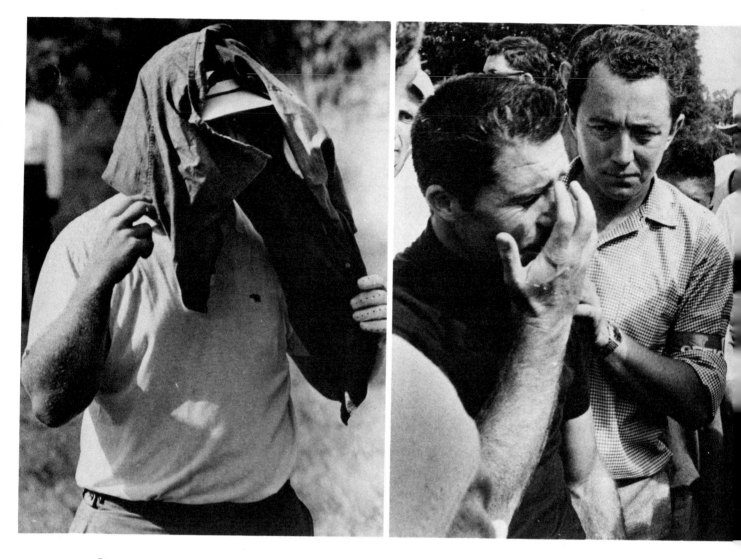

Occupational Hazards

Lightning is the golfer's greatest danger, but ever since this day I've been watchful, too, for things that sting. The occasion was a 1966 exhibition tour in South Africa with Gary Player, and I guess this was just an unlucky hole. The previous day, the head snapped off the driver I'd been using ever since I turned pro, then here we were attacked by a swarm of bees. Gary and I both got tagged a few times, as did many in the gallery, so we decided to give ourselves a couple of pars on the hole and move on—fast.

We were a lot more fortunate, however, than a poor fellow who went down the following day to try to get his dog away from the swarm. I understand both were stung so badly that they later died.

Take Your Choice —
Ball or Club

Australian PGA Championship, Metropolitan Golf Club, Melbourne, 1968. You can see what happened to the five-iron. The ball came out but not very far, and I made an easy six on the hole.

Chances? Slim and None

Bing Crosby National Pro-Am, Monterey Peninsula, 1969. When the tide is out and the wind is up, this is a fairly common scene at the sixteenth at Cypress Point. As you might have guessed, I decided against trying anything fancy, dropped out and took my punishment.

How Do You Play This One? You Tell Me!

Andy Williams San Diego Open, Torrey Pines, 1969. The ball was totally buried, but at least I moved it—backward, to the bottom of the trap. Despite all this, on the way to a closing 73, I managed to win by one shot.

Demonstrators

Like many people in the public eye, I get some crackpot mail and calls, but the scariest incident I have ever been involved in happened at the 1969 PGA Championship at the National Cash Register course in Dayton, Ohio. Apparently, both Gary Player and I, paired together in the third round, were the target of a group of demonstrators who came rushing out onto the course really looking as though they meant business. The scariest thing to me was that I came within a split second of clubbing a man. He was a huge fellow, maybe six feet five inches and around 250 pounds, and he came running straight for me, screaming his head off. Reacting instinctively, I pulled my putter back over my head like an ax, and if he'd come another six inches closer I'd have started the downswing—and I wouldn't have missed. Fortunately, he veered off at the last moment.

Later we learned that the demonstrators weren't planning to harm anyone, but how are you to know that when they are coming for you like an express train? As you can see here, we had a police escort for the rest of the tournament. Sad to say, Gary, because of his nationality, has had to have many such escorts over the years. I have tremendous admiration for his courage in these situations—and his control: he finished second here in Dayton to Raymond Floyd.

146

Who's Winning?

From the look on my face, we're both heading for the water. The tournament was the 1970 U.S. Open at Hazeltine in Minnesota. Considering the way I played that week—I came in forty-ninth, my worst-ever finish in the National Open— I'm sure I got there first.

Remodeling Time Coming Up

U.S. Open, Merion, 1971. I took two shots to get out of this bunker on the second hole of the play-off with Lee Trevino and two more to get out of another one on the next hole. Lee might have won anyhow, because he beat me by three shots, but I determined right then and there to improve my sand play—which I since have, by about a thousand percent.

One problem here was a sand wedge too upright in lie, which placed me too close to the ball, forcing too deep a penetration of the sand. By flattening the lie of the club—and thus the swing—I've found I can consistently graze through the sand at a shallower depth.

148

I Know There's a Golf Course Out There Somewhere! ...

British Open, Royal Birkdale, 1971. Luckily, the ball landed on a road, otherwise I might still be there. Funnily enough, I've never regarded Royal Birkdale as the toughest of the British Open courses, but I've never won there, either. Perhaps this sort of thing is why.

Darn! Those Pine Needles Scratch!

Sahara Invitational, Las Vegas, 1972. Sticky as it looks, I guess this shot must have worked pretty well, because I finished the round with a 66.

149

Occupational Hazards—2

You always hate this to happen to a favorite club, but metal fatigue is inevitable, particularly when a club gets used as much as the driver does. This happened to one of my favorite drivers on the sixteenth hole of the 1972 Tournament of Champions at La Costa. The shaft snapped right between my hands somewhere around impact, the ball went straight down the middle, and all I got was a little bump on the head in the follow-through and a tiny sliver of metal in one of my fingers. That was lucky, because shaft breakage like this in mid-swing can easily rip your hands apart. I was less lucky during the remainder of the tournament, losing to Bobby Mitchell in a play-off.

The hands here, incidentally, belong to Angelo, my caddie. Does he always wear two watches? No, one's mine—Angie always carries it this way for me while I'm playing.

150

Beware Manicures!

I've been fortunate to suffer little injury or illness during most of my career, but here's a wound back in 1972 that could have cost me pretty dearly. I'd won the Masters and the U.S. Open that year, then lost the British Open to Lee Trevino by a shot. Here's what happened when he chipped in on the seventy-first hole and I jammed my finger trying to break his sand wedge!

Much as I felt like doing just that, it isn't what happened, of course. For some unknown reason, I decided to have a manicure while getting my hair trimmed shortly after returning from Britain, and a few days later I came up with a very painful infection under the cuticle, necessitating a couple of hours in the operating theater. The first picture shows me calling home immediately after the surgery, and the second shows an obvious improvement five days later on the Monday prior to the PGA Championship. I can't really blame the injury for my unsuccessful defense at Oakland Hills (Gary Player won), but it didn't help: I played most of the week with the finger off the club, sort of just sticking straight out behind the grip. If I had won the British Open and thereby had a chance at the modern Grand Slam, I might simply have gripped normally and lived with the pain, but there's no question I would have been at a psychological disadvantage, if not a physical one.

Needless to say, I've had no more manicures.

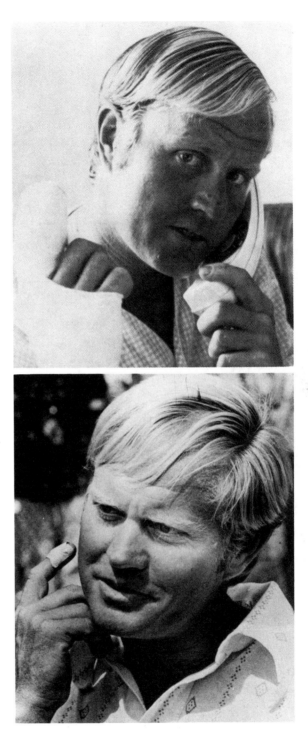

151

How to Make a Quick Seven

Bing Crosby Pro-Am, Monterey Peninsula, 1973. Here's the shot that set up the triple-bogey on seventeen at Cypress Point that I referred to earlier (page 118). The ball (arrow) caught a branch and fell straight down, from where I quietly eased it into a sand trap.

Squelch, Squelch

Here—if you're lucky—is what you get if you're a little short with the pitch on Firestone's "Monster" sixteenth. If you're not lucky, the ball's four feet below water. I started out by taking my shoe and sock off for this shot, but decided I could get a better stance with them on, so put them back again. Made the green too.

Join the Tour and Follow the Sun

No prizes for guessing that this is at the Crosby. The year is 1974, and I think if I'd had any more clothes on, I couldn't have gotten the club above my waist. The other cheery-looking fellows are Gay Brewer (middle) and Gary Player. Fortunately, golf for the day ended right here.

One Too Many = Two Too Many

In all the time I have played golf, I have only once incurred a penalty for having too many clubs in the bag, right here at the Byron Nelson Golf Cassic in 1976.

Fortunately, we discovered the extra club—David Graham's pitching wedge—on the first hole, so the penalty was held to two shots.

The reason this has never happened before is that I make a point of counting my clubs on the first tee before every round and of having my caddie do so too for a double check. Both Angelo and I had done exactly that before this round, and the mystery of how the extra club got in the bag after our check has never been solved. However, David's clubs appear identical to mine, and I had taken a look at his pitching wedge on the way to the tee, then set it down beside his bag. What I suspect happened is that a fan, thinking I'd left my own club behind, stuck it in my bag believing he was doing me a service, but without saying anything about it. Then

153

when he heard about the penalty, he was too embarrassed to speak up.

Here, we're checking particularly thoroughly the next day, even to the point of being sure nothing is hidden beneath the wood covers or the towel. Golf is tough enough without having strokes added that you don't actually hit.

Who's the Guy in the Hat?

U.S. Open, Southern Hills, Tulsa, 1977. I've rarely worn any kind of hat since letting my hair grow, basically because I don't like the "wings" look you see here. But I was getting so sunburned under the eyes at Tulsa, even using a sunscreen (as I do most of the time), that I had to shade myself somehow. My expression just about sums up what sort of tournament it was for me.

Chapter 6
Who Says
I'm Unemotional?

As I said earlier, my public image seems to have veered a full 180 degrees over the past ten years or so, and obviously I'm delighted about that. No doubt my playing record has had a lot to do with the nice way most people now seem to feel about me, but I think I may have helped things along too, simply by growing up a little and getting a bit smarter about life generally. There have been no deliberate or conscious personality changes, but inevitably you change somewhat as you gain experience—for the better, you hope.

Beyond dress, size and hairstyle—which I still believe are pretty superficial factors to judge people by—if I had a problem in my early days, it was a certain one-track-mindedness about the way I played golf. I am by nature a very direct and deliberate sort of fellow, and I guess to some people the way I went about golf in my early days as a pro seemed a little too clinical, a little too machinelike, particularly in contrast to Arnold Palmer. There is no doubt that I knew where I wanted to go and that I intended to get there by the shortest and straightest possible route. Being also by nature a fairly private and not a particularly demonstrative type of person, it simply took me a while to learn that you have to give the fans a little more of yourself than just a golf game. Greater experience and maturity have, I think, allowed me to do that without, I hope, needing to be dishonest or unnatural in my behavior.

One thing I would deny is that I have ever been unemotional about the game of golf as it was actually happening. I may

not roll about on the ground too often or do a Chi Chi Rodriguez number when a putt drops, but I definitely do show what I feel if you care to watch carefully enough. As witness the following. . .

Byron Nelson Golf Classic, Dallas, Texas, 1970

There are certain putts you know are going to just miss as soon as you've hit them, and sometimes they are so close you don't even want to look. Here's one such. Arnold Palmer and I tied with a 274, and I went on to win the play-off.

157

Masters, Augusta, Georgia, 1973

This thirty-foot putt from off the fringe on the eighteenth hole in the final round gave me a 66 and made me, as the TV fellows so love to say, "leader in the clubhouse." I felt as the ball dropped that my 285 might be at least good enough for a play-off, but I was way off base. Tommy Aaron shot a closing 68 to beat it by two.

Atlanta Golf Classic, Georgia, 1973

I started this week with 67-66-66, then did a lot of what you see here in the final round as putts began to slip by instead of dropping from all over as they had the first three days. You don't often win with as high a final round as 73, but I was fortunate to do so here, by two shots over Tom Weiskopf.

158

Masters, Augusta, Georgia, 1974

I didn't win at Augusta National this time, but the shot I made here at the fifteenth in the final round was one of the best recoveries I've ever played. I hit from the very edge of the water almost into the hole. Gary Player took his second green jacket with a two-shot margin over Dave Stockton and Tom Weiskopf.

PGA Championship, Clemmons, North Carolina, 1974

Golf certainly is a game of inches. I missed a birdie here by a fraction of one on the first hole of the final round and ended up losing by a shot to Lee Trevino.

Doral-Eastern Open, Miami, Florida, 1975

A finishing birdie to win by three shots over Forrest Fezler and Bert Yancey. In recent years, I seem to have made a fair number of birdies on final holes, but rarely when I've had to do so to win.

Masters, Augusta, Georgia, 1975

There are putts that you *know* are going to drop the moment they leave the blade. Here's how you feel when they then don't do so. Obviously, others did this week, because I finished up with a fifth win.

Memorial Tournament, Columbus, Ohio, 1976

On the way to a 75 in the second round. This being our first Memorial Tournament, I probably had the same sort of worried look most of the time off the course too. Roger Maltbie beat Hale Irwin in a play-off.

U.S. Open, Atlanta, Georgia, 1976

Laughter is the only way to react to some of the things that happen in golf, because if you didn't laugh, you'd cry. The other gesture is one I'm told I often make. As seen here, it's usually accompanied by a rather rude noise. Finishing tied eleventh, I probably made many such noises that week. This was Jerry Pate's championship, of course.

161

Jackie Gleason Inverrary Classic, Lauderhill, Florida, 1977

Three putts on the first green is always a disgusting way to begin a round. But things got better: an eagle on the fifteenth gave me a five-shot lead—and a repeat win in my own "backyard."

Masters, Augusta, Georgia, 1977

Despite these histrionics, I shot one of my best-ever finishing rounds in a major, a 66. Unfortunately for me, Tom Watson played equally as well for a 67 and a two-shot victory.

Tournament of Champions, Carlsbad, California, 1977

As so often happens, the chip rimmed the cup and then I missed the return putt. Even so, I managed to scramble into a play-off with Bruce Lietzke and birdie the third extra hole for my sixty-second U.S. tour win, tying Ben Hogan's total. I added the Memorial Tournament in May for number sixty-three, but I'm still a long way off Sam Snead's record of eighty-four.

Chapter 7
Some Friends and
Contemporaries

Arnold Palmer

I'm often asked how friendly Arnold and I have really been over the years. The short answer is we've been as good friends as two guys ever could be who've tried as hard and as often as we have to beat each other and who are as different as we are in non-golfing tastes and interests. What I would like to add is that it was Arnold who first made a pleasant personal relationship possible by his graciousness when I first showed up on the scene. Obviously, then he was the king and I was the fellow kick-ing the throne. Candidly, I thought his handling of that situation was nothing short of terrific and a perfect example of the human qualities that have so contrib-uted to his popularity. Looking back now, I have even greater respect for those qual-ities, because I am not sure that in a simi-lar situation I could be quite as gracious as he was at that time.

Talking about friendship prompts a word about how it works on the tour gen-erally. Although I haven't had experience in other pro sports, I can't imagine one with more genuine camaraderie among the players than golf. Almost everyone in the game is "friendly," in the sense that there is very little apparent enmity among the players. If there are antagonisms or jealousies or other forms of negative emotion, they are rarely displayed, not only to the public but within the tour fraternity itself.

Essentially, all of us are individualists who respect and defend a common right to do our best without interference from others who are doing the same. Everyone pulls for himself, but without actively pulling against anyone else. Obviously, what makes such a happy climate possible is the absence of direct man-to-man conflict inherent in stroke-play golf and the absence of a profit motive beyond that of each individual for his own direct account. If we competed in match play every week and/or were "owned" as team-sport players are, things might be different. Also contributing to the general amiability, of course, is the individual's interest in the group welfare of what in essence is something between an exclusive club and a large family.

Much as it promotes camaraderie and casual companionship, however, the tour isn't conducive to the formation of very deep friendships. For one thing, most of the players are pretty individualistic; and for another, the life is too unsettled and nomadic to easily nurture deep relationships. There are some good pals out there, but that's about as far as it goes for most players.

I recognized this very early in my career, which, combined with a strong in-

herited sense and love of family, is what has made me seek both to have Barbara and the children with me as much as possible on tour and to be home with them as often and for as long as possible when I'm not on the tour. I make an effort to be as friendly as I naturally can be with everyone on the tour, and to the best of my knowledge I don't have any enemies out there. But, with a few exceptions, neither do I have any relationships quite as close as those that have formed in my other, non-tour lives. Most tour players, I think, are much the same.

Getting back to Arnold, it really would have been almost impossible not to become pretty friendly when spending as much time traveling and playing together as we did for seven or eight years. The best way I can summarize it is to say that we both had tremendous fun trying to beat each other's brains out and that we had even more fun when taking our breathers together.

Here's an example of the latter. Somehow both of us had ended up at a music spot following a round in the Bob Hope Desert Classic, and everyone was having a great time, when Arnold decided he had to go to the bathroom. On the way back, he happened to brush by a young lady and, much to her horror, knocked her wig off. Arnold grabbed it and stuck it on his head, and for some crazy reason I rushed over and gave him a big kiss on the cheek and dragged him onto the dance floor.

168

Then, after we'd danced a while, Arnold decided he should lead and stuck the wig on me. Believe it or not, I'd only had a couple of drinks. Of course, everybody there loved it because it was so supposedly out of character for me to do a thing like that.

Looks like I'd just cracked a funny—Arnie and I have always done a lot of joking and ribbing together. We were all dolled up for the Metropolitan Golf Writers Awards Dinner in 1972, where Arnie, Ben Hogan, Walter Hagen, Bobby Jones and myself were cited as "all-time golfing greats."

Gary Player

Gary was the top money-winner on the U.S. tour the year before I joined it and, if not quite the king that Arnold was, very much the pretender to the throne. Like Arnold, he was very friendly, gracious and helpful to me right from the start, and we rapidly formed a close friendship that was soon to extend also to our families. These relationships have flourished over the years, even though we no longer spend a lot of time together. One reason why they have, of course, is our similar values and interests. Basically, both Gary and I are deeply involved in the activities of our families and take a keen delight in good health and the active, outdoor life that promotes it. That, plus an ability to rib and be ribbed about our respective foibles (like the fact that his waist measurement was at one time only two inches bigger than my thigh circumference), allows us to be totally relaxed in each other's company both on and off the golf course.

Much as he's admired here in the States, I don't think many American fans fully appreciate Gary's true stature as a golfer and an athlete. With the exception of Sam Snead, no one has played as well for as long as he has: 1978 will be his twenty-sixth year of professional tournament golf, most of it at the very summit of the game.

Eight major-championship wins are the obvious highlights of that career, but even more impressive to me is the sheer *breadth* of his accomplishments: Gary has won tournaments not once but *repeatedly* in just about every country where golf is played professionally. Certainly no other golfer has approached his total (through 1977) of 110 tournament victories around the world, and I'd find it hard to believe that any other sports figure has traveled more miles than he has or spent so many nights away from home. All this has been achieved with very little natural talent for the game or financial resource initially, the smallest build of any great player since Gene Sarazen, and a constant escalation in non-golfing emotional pressures arising from his South African nationality, including receiving periodic threats of violence. It's a heck of a record, and he's a heck of a guy in every respect.

The picture here is one of my favorites: Gary helping me on with the green jacket following the 1975 Masters. He had, of course, won for the second time at Augusta the previous year.

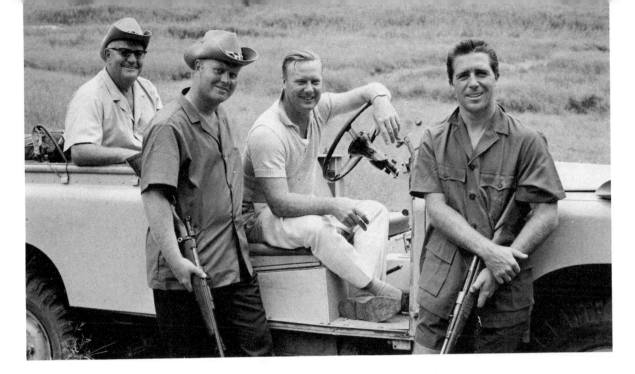

Back in 1966, Gary invited Barbara and me to see and enjoy South Africa, with some golf thrown in on the side. Both Barbara's and my parents came along, and all of us had a great seventeen-day vacation with the Players, slightly clouded in my case only by Gary's defeating me in the six-round challenge match we played. The fishing was as marvelous as our host had promised, and we also did a little bit of hunting during our visits to the game reserves. The fellows in the Jeep are my father and, at the wheel, our guide, Mike Rattray, owner of Mala Mala, one of the game reserves we visited.

Gene Sarazen

Gene's heyday was well before my time, but we've become good friends over the years, and I'm delighted to have seen him emerge more and more a statesman of the game in recent times.

He certainly was one heck of a golfer for his size, and I'd have to believe from what I've been told that he was also probably the most combative of all the great champions. The remarkable thing about him today is his physical condition: he's well into his seventies but probably in better shape than most fifty-year-olds—and still playing par golf too. Here, we're playing together in the 1971 PGA Championship.

Ben Hogan

I first really became acquainted with Ben when we were paired together in the last two rounds of the 1960 U.S. Open at Cherry Hills, which we both had a chance to win right up to the final holes. I had, of course, heard all the stuff about how cold and aloof he was, so the reality was a delightful surprise as well as a memorable golfing experience. He didn't say a whole lot beyond "Good shot," and that only when you hit a *truly* good shot, but no one could have been pleasanter to play with. Despite my youth and comparative inexperience, he treated me from the word go as a fellow competitor and with an obvious if unstated respect for the fact that I was there in contention alongside him. He was totally considerate in observing the etiquette of the game and the situation. Above all, he was friendly without being effusive, which, not being too hot on effusiveness myself, immediately made me like him as an individual. In short, it was a very enjoyable experience, as have been all my other contacts with him.

Every year at the Masters thereafter when he was still playing, even when I was still an amateur, he would seek me out and suggest, "Jack, how about a game?" Jollying it up with the herd may not have been Ben's scene, but with people he likes and respects he is a very pleasant companion—and, of course, the most inspirational companion one could ever hope to have on the golf course itself.

Winners of All Four Majors

The four of us here are the only golfers who have won all four modern majors—the Masters, the U.S. and British Opens, and the PGA Championship. The other gentlemen are, of course, from the left, Gene Sarazen, Ben Hogan and Gary Player. Gary has only to win the U.S. Open again to join me as a two-time winner of all four. The picture was taken at the Westchester Country Club—obviously when double-breasted jackets were in style!

Bob Jones

I've talked already about what Bob Jones has meant to me, both on and off the golf course. This picture of us, taken at the 1966 Masters, is one of my favorites.

173

Sam Snead

I think I was about thirty years old before Sam finally stopped calling me "Junior," but despite that he's one of my favorite people in golf. I've played with him a lot over the years, and the more I've gotten to know him, the better I've liked him. Certainly, he can be a little rough around the edges at times with people he doesn't know or like, but he has a very big heart—much bigger than most people would believe from the look on his face at times. He is also one of the funniest men I've ever met, a great mimic and a marvelous storyteller—an absolute riot when he's in the mood. His athleticism, of course, is incredible: there simply would be no contest if they ever gave an award for who has played a sport the best the longest.

Apart from enjoying the man himself, I like to play with him because of his effect on my game. You can't help trying to mimic that marvelous rhythm, and I don't think there has ever been a time when my tempo hasn't improved after having played with Sam.

The picture was taken during the 1969 U.S. Open at Champions in Houston. Seems I was even copying Sam's style of walking!

Byron Nelson

They say Byron was the straightest golfer who ever lived, and although I never played with him competitively, I

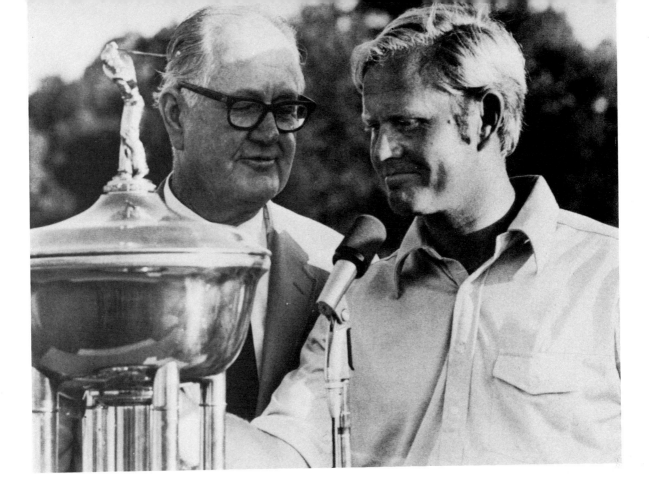

can believe it from an exhibition I saw him give back in 1954. It was at the Los Angeles Country Club for a group of youngsters, and he just about knocked the caddie down on every shot—his straightness was literally incredible. Certainly, no one I've ever played with has hit the ball as consistently straight as he did that day.

One thing I've always admired about Byron is how he has handled himself as a top player: you'll never meet a more straightforward and unassuming man. Here, he's giving me the trophy for winning his tournament, the Byron Nelson Golf Classic, in Dallas in 1970. I beat Arnie in a sudden-death play-off.

Tony Lema

Tony and I became good friends when we played together for the United States in the 1965 World Cup at Club de Campo in Madrid, the first time I'd played in Spain. The previous year, Tony had beaten me with some incredible golf in a four-day gale at St. Andrews to win the British Open on his first visit to Great Britain, coming straight off a win in the States and with only one and a half rounds of practice on the Old Course (shook the Scots right down to their toenails, that did).

He'd been out on the tour for five or six years by then, and everyone out there knew he was one of the most talented men ever to play the game. But his early record reflected his free-spirited bachelor life. Once he got married, he quickly took his rightful place in golf, and it is a great tragedy that he didn't live to fully savor his success after the very tough times of his youth. He and his wife were killed in a private-plane crash on the way to an exhibition in 1966.

Here we are not long before that happened wading off the course when play was called while jointly leading in the final round of the New Orleans Open.

Lee Trevino

Lee was my playing partner in the final round of the 1972 U.S. Open at Pebble Beach. Typical of him, he looked happier about my win than I did as we came off the last green.

He is a great fellow: honest, straightforward, very hardworking, a great competitor. His response to the back injury that has hit his career so hard the past couple of years is characteristic of the man: no complaining or excuse-making—just a lot of very hard rebuilding work and a deep determination to get to the top again. I really hope he makes it. Lee likes his fun, but don't let the clowning fool you. There's a very serious and intelligent man behind it, and a very good one.

Tom Weiskopf and
Johnny Miller

This picture was taken as we waited for the prize presentation following the 1975 Masters, and the expressions reflect the outcome. It was the fourth time Tom had been runner-up at Augusta, and the second time for Johnny. I'm convinced both will win more than once there in the future, because to me they are the two most naturally talented golfers of the era. Both are tall, very strong, swing the club marvelously, possess every shot in the bag and are highly intelligent. Only certain temperamental factors have occasionally

held them back so far, and it's my experience that these factors change with maturity. All the stuff you read in the papers and magazines about them being "finished" because they have a bad season or two is garbage. Both have all the talent necessary to achieve any goals they care to set themselves in golf.

Tom and I have always played a lot of golf together, but we have become close friends in recent years through our shared love of fishing and hunting. He isn't anything like the ogre some of the press make him out to be. Certainly, he has trouble hiding his feelings at times, but in terms of personal friendships, his absolute hon-

178

esty is one of his most attractive traits. You may not always care for it, but at least you always know exactly where you stand with Tom! As a golfer, he has not only a marvelous natural swing but one that in my view will last as long as he wants to keep playing. Consequently, it's my belief that his best years are still ahead of him.

I don't know Johnny as well as I know Tom, which may be why his recent play is such an enigma to me. I can understand a fellow with his talent getting a little bit off his game at times, but, frankly, getting as far off as he appears to have been in the past couple of years is beyond my comprehension. My guess at his problem is that he hasn't as yet been able to work out a formula that allows him to balance the various compartments of his life—most notably his keen desire for privacy and a full family life—to his total emotional satisfaction. In other words, what he feels to be a clash of conflicting interests and obligations may affect his desire and concentration at times on the golf course. But given time, he's certainly smart and stable enough to resolve these concerns, and when he does he could whip the world with all that talent.

Tom Watson

It was a refreshing change, after the kind of year we'd both had, for Tom and me to play *for* instead of against each other, as we were doing here in the 1977 Ryder Cup matches in September at Royal Lytham and St. Anne's.

I don't think there can be any question that Tom is only at the beginning of a great career in golf. He isn't, in my estimation, quite as naturally talented physically as Weiskopf and Miller, but he sure makes up for that in a lot of other ways. Perhaps the most impressive of these are his self-confidence, his maturity and his tremendous determination. Tom knows where he wants to go, and he's going there in the straightest possible line and the shortest possible time—almost to the point of having blinkers on. That reminds me somewhat of myself at around his age. He has another notable attribute, which is that he is a very pleasant and level-headed fellow who won't let all the things that come with success change his personality or destroy his sense of values. I sense he'll also closely protect his private life, which is an important consideration for any athlete who reaches the top.

Chapter 8
Other Names
You'll Know

HRH King Leopold of Belgium

British Open, Royal Lytham and St. Anne's, England, 1963. I threw this championship away by bogeying the last two holes to miss a play-off with Bob Charles and Phil Rodgers by one shot (Charles won, the only left-hander to capture a major so far). Ex-King Leopold and his wife, Princess Liliane de Rethy, followed me for most of the second round, and we became quite well-acquainted thereafter, to the point of still keeping in contact. Both were extremely enthusiastic golfers, and good ones too. Here (with a security man on the left), they are watching me try to figure out a birdie putt on the eighteenth green. I didn't.

183

The Duke of Windsor

Canada Cup (now World Cup), St. Nom de la Bretèche, Paris, France, 1963. The Duke had been a very keen golfer for many years, and living mainly in Paris as he then did, he followed the play every day during this Canada Cup. I'm afraid I rather shook him up at one point. On the seventh hole during one of the rounds, I got myself into a very deep, cavernous greenside bunker and hit the ball out blind straight into the hole. The shot so surprised the Duke that he fell backward off his shooting stick. Fortunately, he wasn't hurt and seemed as amused by the incident as everyone else. With us here, of course, are Gary Player and my teammate, Arnold Palmer.

President Eisenhower

Philadelphia, Pa., 1963. I met and greatly enjoyed talking with President Ike at a number of golf events, but unfortunately never got to play with him. We were scheduled to play together a couple of times, including a Heart Fund exhibition on the day this picture was taken, but his health prevented him from taking part on both occasions. He was, of course, about as enthusiastic a golfer as there's ever been, and he made an enormous contribution to the growth of the game in this country just by playing as often as he did when President. In fact, it's been said that Ike, Arnie and TV were the three factors that initially got most of today's fifteen or so million American players out onto golf courses. On a personal basis, the President was a most charming man and an unusual one to me in that he was always much more interested in what *you* were doing than in talking about his own activities. I think he was genuinely interested in people, as well as eager to know what was going on in worlds other than his own.

James Garner

American Cancer Society Exhibition, Scioto Country Club, Columbus, Ohio, 1965. This event was our first effort at trying to bring some top golf to Columbus. Jim Garner and Bob Hope came in and played a round at Scioto with me and the pro there, Walker Inman, and the support was fantastic—we raised $35,000 for the Cancer Society that one day. Out of this developed the Columbus Pro-Am in aid of the Children's Hospital, which ran very successfully for ten years, and out of that grew the idea for what in 1976 became the Memorial Tournament.

Jim around that time was about a one- or two-handicap golfer, and he's still one of the best players in the entertainment industry. We all had a lot of fun, including Barbara, who was then due with our third child. That hadn't stopped her from walking and riding around the course, and as she seemed to be feeling fine, I invited the fellows over to the house for dinner. I knew Barb was eager to get the meal going, and after a while she asked me to fix the fire while she prepared the steaks. Everybody was very relaxed, and I told her not to be in so much of a hurry and that I'd do it as soon as we'd played a game of pool. About half an hour later, she asked me again about fixing the fire, and I said, "In a minute, Barbara, in a minute. There's no hurry." About half an hour after that, she yelled down again: "Okay, the fire's fixed. The steaks are done. Dinner's ready." I felt a little guilty, but nothing compared with what came later.

186

As we were finishing eating, Barb excused herself and disappeared for about forty-five minutes. Eventually, I began to realize that maybe she wasn't feeling too well and went looking for her. She was in the back room with her coat on and a suitcase in her hand. "Well," she greeted me, "it's all taken care of. I've called the doctor, the baby's on the way, and I've got everything packed. Now, do you think you might *possibly* get me to the hospital?"

I moved pretty fast, but not as fast as Hope and Garner. You've never seen a couple of guys scatter out of a house so quick in your life.

On our way to the hospital, we decided to call the baby Robert James for our two friends if it was a boy. She wasn't, and we called our new daughter Nancy Jean.

Del Webb and Dinah Shore

Sahara Invitational, Las Vegas, Nevada, 1966. This picture reminds me of an interesting experience—the strongest wind I ever played golf in—and also of an unusual Christmas present.

Del Webb was a great supporter of mine in my early days as a pro and a man I came to have great respect for the more I got to know him and the amazing story behind his success. His right-hand man, Herb McDonald, who started and ran the Sahara Invitational for many years, also quickly became a close personal friend (as well as in later years the man who got the Memorial Tournament off the ground and running like clockwork). Herb always wanted me to win the Sahara, not only because we

were pals but because he liked the effect on pre-tournament ticket sales of my being certain to defend. Anyway, on this occasion, I started reasonably enough with a 71; and then on the morning of the second day, the wind came up like nothing I've ever encountered before or since: 75 to 80 mph—hurricane force. Inevitably, of course, down there in the desert, it was as much a sandstorm as a windstorm, and conditions were unbelievably difficult—I don't remember which was tougher, standing or seeing. Somehow I got through all this with a 77, but felt that the wind would be bound to drop later in the day and that I'd blown myself—or, rather, been blown—right out of the tournament. Meeting Herb after the round for a little bass fishing up at Lake Mead, I told him how terrible I felt my score was and added, just to have him share my frustration, "And it won't do you any good, either, because now some donkey will go out and win your tournament, and you'll have a tough time selling tickets next

year." But Herb didn't seem too bothered, and when we got back from a nice afternoon at the lake, I found out why. Having lived in the desert for many years, he knew its weather patterns inside out. The wind had not died down as I'd anticipated, my 77 proved to be one of the best scores of the day, and I went on to shoot 68-66 and win the tournament. When Herb presented me with the winner's check, he smilingly said, "Nice going, donkey!" So when Christmas came around that year, we found the perfect gift for Herb—yes, you've guessed it, a donkey.

I believe Dinah Shore was working at the Sahara that year, and she graciously came out to make the presentation. Since then, of course, she's made a fine contribution to the women's game with her big Palm Springs event in collaboration with Colgate-Palmolive.

Here are Herb and I on a calmer day that same year in Las Vegas.

Bart Starr

Tournament of Champions, Las Vegas, Nevada, 1967. Being a regular at Ohio State and Miami Dolphin games whenever I'm not on the road, I've met a lot of football players and liked most of them. Here's one of the nicest guys I've ever had the pleasure of meeting—Bart exemplifies just about everything I'd like to see my sons grow up to be.

Athletes All

NBC Academy Awards of Sports, Los Angeles, California, 1968. Johnny Carson an athlete? Well, he's a heck of a tennis player, they tell me! Johnny was emceeing the TV show, which offered an enjoyable opportunity to talk with other sportsmen. They are, from the right, Bob Pettit, Daryl Lamonica, Willie Shoemaker, Johnny Unitas and, between Carson and myself, Carl Yazstremski. Willie had obviously just fallen off a horse. I think by this point in the evening, I was eager to fall out of those clothes—they are not my favorite getup.

Andy Williams

Andy Williams–San Diego Open, Torrey Pines, California, 1969. Being of slight build—it's interesting how many top entertainers are—Andy has distance problems with golf, but that doesn't diminish his enthusiasm for the game. He's a quiet fellow who cherishes his privacy, but he's made a big contribution to golf with his longtime support of the San Diego tournament. I guess my big smile here was for the big first-place check.

190

HRH Prince Bertil of Sweden

Volvo Open, Stockholm, Sweden, 1970. The Prince and I had a most enjoyable round together in the pro-am, following which I finished second in the tournament proper to longtime French champion Jean Garaialde. Although I think I was a bit more clothes-conscious by then, I took a lot of ribbing in the Swedish press that week for my "short pants." Then as now, the "in" style in Europe was to wear trousers well down over the shoes. Apparently, my pants only just reached my ankles, and the Swedish cartoonists had a lot of fun with that. Almost every day, they'd tell their readers: "It's easy to recognize Nicklaus, the American. He's the fellow in the short pants."

Bob Hope and Jackie Gleason

World Cup, Palm Beach Gardens, Florida, 1971. I imagine a lot of fans sometimes wonder about Lee Trevino's legendary humor: is he really as naturally funny as he seems or is it a deliberate, rehearsed act? Well, all I can say is, when I've been around he has never failed to pass what I would regard as the ultimate test for a genuine comedian, which is to hold his own with the top professionals of the laughter business. Here we are with Jackie Gleason and Bob Hope in a typical situation. We were just about to play in the World Cup Pro-Am, and the subject of conversation was the size of the bets. Bob and Jackie could hardly even get so much as a word in!

All three of these gentlemen have been good friends of mine in recent years, and Bob for a lot longer than that. As all the world knows, of course, he's a great supporter of the game through his tournament and charity activity as well as being a total nut about playing it. We've helped each other frequently over the years by bending our schedules in order to play charity-oriented pro-ams and exhibitions in which one or the other of us has had an interest, as have Jackie and I also. Both are fun to play with, and hilarious when their very serious golfing rivalry gets the needles sharpened—which is always, I guess.

John D. MacArthur and Fred Corcoran

World Cup, PGA National, Palm Beach Gardens, Florida, 1971. I guess if you're one of the wealthiest men in the world, as

Mr. MacArthur was, you can do things exactly as you want to, and that's how John D. always was during the time I knew him, often to the infuriation of people who had to deal with him in business but whom he didn't particularly take a shine to personally. He was a very unusual individual in every respect, but I always enjoyed him, and he seemed to become very fond of me and also of Lee Trevino. I think he liked our straightforwardness and, of course, in Lee's case his humor—who wouldn't?

It's a shame the PGA and John D. couldn't work things out over the PGA National facility, because it was a marvelous setup for the association, but there were some pretty rugged personality conflicts as well as business problems. Typically, the facility—now the John D. MacArthur National—prospered as a resort/real estate development under Mr. Mac's direct command.

Fred Corcoran, seen here with us on the right, ran the World Cup for many years until his death from a stroke in June 1977, but that was only one of at least a dozen major contributions he made to golf around the world. Fred was totally devoted to the game, and although he never gave an outward impression of working very hard, his output was tremendous, especially as manager and promoter-in-chief of the men's tour from 1936 to 1947 and later as founder and orchestrator of the women's tour. Everybody involved in the operation of golf used Fred as an encyclopedia on the game, as much for the human and humorous stories in which he always wrapped facts and figures as for the information itself. He had an anecdote about everything and everybody from way back in his Boston caddie days right up to the previous week's tournament. He'll be very much missed all over the world.

John Newcombe

Wimbledon, England, 1971. Loving tennis as much as I do and with Wimbledon immediately preceding the British Open, I'd made a habit for years of getting over there early enough to watch the finals on BBC television between practice rounds. This was my first visit to the actual tournament itself, and I fell so in love with the place and its Masters-like atmosphere, as well as the tennis, that I've taken to stopping off there for at least one afternoon on most British Open trips since.

John had just won the men's singles for the second year in a row when we posed for this picture. I've always liked the down-to-earthness of Aussies, and I found him typical of them—a very nice fellow with absolutely no affectations or airs. With us here, from the left, standing, are my business partner at that time, Put Pierman; one of my financial consultants, Jerry Halperin, of Cooper Lybrand; and an old and dear British friend, "Buzzer" Haddingham, who ran Slazengers for many years. Buzzer was and is a top official at Wimbledon, which is how we came by our tickets—they are even tougher to obtain than Masters badges!

194

Glen Campbell

Glen Campbell—Los Angeles Open, Riviera Country Club, California, 1972. Glen has always been one of my favorite singers and one of my favorite people among the show-biz crowd. When he's out on a course, he's out there for golf, not for self-promotion. And his play shows it— he's been as low as a two-handicap when he's had time to work at the game.

It's often said that there's a lot of "heart" in show biz, and Glen certainly proved that as far as I am concerned in 1977. We had invited a lot of celebrities to the first Memorial Tournament Pro-Am in 1976, but Glen hadn't been able to make it because of work commitments. At the Tournament Players Championship early in 1977, he told me how sorry he was to have missed the event and said he'd very much like to come and play that May. As we had decided to cut back on the celebrity side of things, this was a little embarrassing, but I explained the situation as best I could. "Forget the celebrity bit," said Glen. "I'd just like to come along and play as an amateur, and if you'd like it, I'd also like to bring the group and give you a show for the pro-am dinner." "Glen," I told him, "you just made me an offer I can't refuse." So he did exactly that, putting on a super show to wind up the pre-tournament festivities and seeking absolutely nothing for it in return.

195

Prime Minister Tanaka

Tokyo, Japan, 1972. The fact that the country's prime minister would invite me out to play a round of golf with him is indicative of how deeply in love with the game so many Japanese are. We had a lot of fun despite the language barrier—and the endless cacophony of clicking cameras.

Looks as though the prime minister is releasing with the wrists a little early here, but what he lacked in form he made up for in enthusiasm. That's true of most Japanese amateurs, as exemplified by the almost unbelievably high cost of club golf membership over there and the enormous traffic at the country's thousands of driving ranges. Many of these are triple- and double-deckers and almost all are floodlit. At the busiest times—from 9 P.M. to 1 A.M. on weekdays and all day on weekends—players often have to wait up to two or three hours for a booth. Supplementing the public facilities, many office buildings in the big cities have caged mini-ranges on their roofs for employees.

John McKay

Bob Hope Desert Classic, Palm Springs, California, 1973. This won't be too popular a picture among my Columbus friends, because USC had just annihilated Ohio State in the Rose Bowl. Despite that, John and I had a lot of fun playing together—with, as I recall, Woody Hayes a prime topic of conversation. Like Woody and just about all the other top football coaches I've met, I found John a very positive and confident person. But I think I must have gotten to him a little, because the following year Ohio State annihilated USC!

President Ford

Tournament Players Championship, Inverrary, Florida, 1974. This was the first time I had played golf with a President, and I guess it must have inspired me, because I somehow shot a 63 despite all the hoopla and backchat going on between our other two pro-am partners, Bob Hope and Jackie Gleason.

Since then, I've played quite a lot of golf with President Ford and have developed a very enjoyable friendship with him off the course too. Obviously, with all the experiences he has had, he is a fascinating man to talk with. Golf is, of course, his favorite summer sport—every time I see him, he's dropped his handicap another stroke or two. But, like me, he's a lover of all sports. In fact, we were planning to do some skiing together at the time I was working on this book. Given the time, there's no doubt he could get down to a low handicap because he's a very athletic man—well up with me off the tee anytime he catches one flush. Socially, he's such a kindly and natural fellow that you are always completely at ease with him. Typical of his kindliness was his offer to let us have one of the pups of his golden retriever, Liberty, when Barbara or I mentioned we were currently without a family dog and how much we liked the breed. Her name is Lady; she arrived around Thanksgiving of 1977, and she's a beauty.

Peter Falk

Glen Campbell–Los Angeles Open, Riviera Country Club, California, 1976. Here's an enthusiastic golfer if ever there was one—as intense about the game as he is on the screen, and not a bad player,

either. Actually, what fascinated me about playing with Peter was that he talks exactly the same way in normal conversation as he does in "Colombo," which makes you wonder when he's going to put on that rumpled raincoat.

Perry Como

Stuart, Florida, 1972. Perry is one of those people, fairly rare in show business, whom you love to be around because he's so totally natural and undemonstrative. He lived only four or five houses away from us in Florida for several years, but there was never anything to make you notice that one of the world's top entertainers was just down the block. His golf swing is as mellow as the man himself. Wish I could be as easygoing!

198

Evel Knievel

Bob Hope Desert Classic, Palm Springs, California, 1976. I don't know how or why Evel got into the stunt business, but it's my guess he would have succeeded at just about anything he tried that took guts and nerve, because he's got more of both than any ten other guys I've ever met. When he isn't breaking himself into small pieces, he's usually playing golf for huge sums of money—he makes most of the game's so-called hustlers look like penny pinochle players. Unfortunately, his game isn't always quite as big as his betting, but he's the ultimate golf nut, win or lose. The day we played in the Hope, he was so keen for his family to meet me, he flew them down from Montana in the morning and then back that night just to walk around the course with us!

Bing Crosby

Memorial Tournament, Columbus, Ohio, 1976. There's never been a nicer guy than Bing Crosby, and I can't imagine there will ever be another entertainer with quite his popularity and presence in golf. As the founder of the pro-entertainer format with his own tournament back in the thirties, he was, of course, the first of all today's show-business sponsors, but he was much more than that. Never in my experience of him did Bing use the game for self-exploitation or even for self-promotion if he could possibly avoid it. If he got involved in a golfing activity, it was essentially for fun and to promote the game—any personal benefits that came his way went directly to charity. Close friends of his have told me that he did his best all through his life, as much as he could, to keep golf a part of his private life and away from his professional activities. He was an excellent player—good enough to compete in both the U.S. and the British Amateur championships—but you never heard him talk about his own game. When he did talk about golf generally, it was with profound knowledge and deep insight and an obvious great love for the human and sporting values and standards the game so uniquely expresses.

To be less serious about Bing, I guess the story of my greatest single embarrassment in life bears repeating. My birthday usually falls during the Crosby, and one time long ago during the tournament, before I knew Bing well, I got a call from a mutual friend, John Swanson, asking me

199

to have an evening drink with the guys. I told John I was too tired, but before I could put the phone down, he said, "Well, hang on a minute, because I've got a fellow here who wants to say hello to you." Suddenly, there is another voice on the phone, singing "Happy birthday to you, happy birthday to you...," and I'm thinking, Who in the heck is *this* guy... what's *with* this character? So after he finished, I cleared my throat and gave him a very businesslike "To whom am I speaking, please?"—using my best flat, oh-yeah, who-cares telephone voice (which is still with me, I'm afraid). So there's a pause, and then the voice says, "This is

Bing Crosby, Jack. Happy birthday. Well, I guess I *was* a bit hoarse, wasn't I?" We kidded about it often afterward, but never without my feeling a hot flush crawling up my neck.

With Bing here, on his left, is another close friend and longtime supporter, John Galbreath, Columbus entrepreneur, owner of the Pittsburgh Pirates, and at various times also owner of the world's top racehorses. Memorial Tournament co-chairman Bob Hoag is driving the golf cart, and next to him is Larry O'Brien, who handles the tournament press facility and also my own press relations out of our North Palm Beach office.

200

Andy Warhol

Ohio Kings Island Open, Cincinnati, Ohio, 1977. Andy lives in a world very different from mine, and I enjoyed meeting him all the more for that. I found him extremely professional: very quiet and pleasant and totally on top of the job he was doing. He was taking my photograph for a collection of paintings of sportsmen that he was putting together. The shots he took of me were all in basically the same pose but with different Warhol backgrounds. There were to be eight paintings of each of six sportsmen, and each of us received one for posing.

HRH Princess Alexandra

Ryder Cup, Royal Lytham and St. Anne's, England, 1977. I don't believe the Princess plays golf—very few members of the British royal family do at the present time—but she appeared to enjoy herself very much at the Ryder Cup matches. She seemed very "with it" to me. We had been told that she wouldn't sign autographs, but she said, "Pooh, pooh to that stuff!" and signed a whole bunch of them. I found it very easy and enjoyable to talk to her, and she made some extremely funny observations that you probably wouldn't expect from a princess. Looking on here are U.S. captain Dow Finsterwald (next to the Princess), Dave Stockton and Ed Sneed.

Chapter 9
From the
Family Album

Here's a whole lot of beef! My dad (left), at about 230 pounds, and my Uncle Frank, at about 260 pounds, make me, at 210 pounds, look small by comparison. We're all bundled up for a rare cold day at the Masters in the early 1960s. Dad and my uncle never missed my first tee shot in all the years they went to Augusta together. Frank, my father's older brother, still comes to the Masters every year and to as many other tournaments as he can manage. Like my dad, he's an entirely self-made man: a dentist in Bath, New York, a small town in the Finger Lakes region. I don't know about the popularity of dentists generally, but this one is certainly well-liked, because he was mayor of that town for something like sixteen years.

All our kids have always loved sports. Jackie was twenty-one months here, but he could throw a football almost as soon as he could walk. These days he still plays everything in season, but football has become his number-one game after golf.

A backyard snapshot on Nan's second birthday, in 1967. The kids are all cleaned and combed and obviously not enjoying it very much. In fact, it amazes me that we ever got them to hold that still. Steve, then four, is on the left and Jack, coming up on six, on the right.

My father died February 19, 1970, from cancer of the pancreas and liver. This picture, the last one of the family group with him, was taken the previous Christmas. My sister and her husband, Howard Hutchinson, are immediately behind my dad.

My father continued to have the greatest influence of anyone in my life right up to his death, and following it I made a new resolve to live as he had guided me and to try to meet the goals that I know he wanted me to attain, both in golf and elsewhere. I am still trying to do that.

Golf's never grabbed Steve quite as it has Jack, and he's very much a streak player: 77 one day and 97 the next. But the resources are there should he ever decide to take the game seriously, because he is naturally athletic and possesses exceptionally good coordination. There isn't a sport he can't play reasonably well just by instinct, and at those he likes best— football, basketball, baseball and tennis— he shows real talent. We also think he has considerable academic potential should he ever head that way, although studying hasn't been too strongly favored up to now. As with Jack at the same age, Steve's not too hot on instruction from the old man. He listens, but then generally goes and does things his own way. What sometimes irritates me is how well it works. Here, he's playing in Columbus in 1972, aged nine.

We showed Gary's swing on pages 126–27. Here's how he learned it—keeping me company on the practice tee at Lost Tree. By the look on his face, he just fanned one.

We like to take the same family-group photograph every Christmas to make a record of how five of us are growing up and two of us are growing older. Here's the 1973 edition.

I've never had much of a problem saying no to people. Barb's the opposite. She can't say no to anyone, ever. Wherever we go and whatever we do, she has to spend all her time making sure everyone else is happy, often to the point of exhausting herself. Leave a hotel and you have to allow at least half an hour for her to say goodbye to everyone—the cook, the waiters, the receptionist, the maids, the bellboys, the whole shebang. She forever puts others ahead of herself, is forever thoughtful. I'm pretty good on names, but she's phenomenal—she probably remembers the name of everyone she's ever met everywhere in the world. Thankfully, people instinctively recognize her good nature and rarely take advantage of it. Generally, as you see on previous page at the 1974 PGA Championship, it's a pleasant word and maybe an autograph. But she's certainly made a great number of friends for both of us through the years with her patience and kindliness.

When it comes to having a marriage partner, I am certainly one of the lucky ones.

Like all the gang, Nan is athletic—in fact, maybe the best all-around athlete in the family. I guess her best sport currently is tennis, but she plays so many it's difficult to keep up with her. In addition to tennis, she currently plays volleyball and soccer for the school teams, and I don't think a sport or game has been invented that she hasn't tried. If there is one and she discovers it, she will definitely try it and probably do well at it too. Here, she's at a school swim meet in 1975. She's not a regular on the swim team now, but not long ago they asked her to fill in for a girl who was ill. Typically, she chose the

toughest event she could find, the medley, swam all four strokes and placed second. Golf is about the only game she doesn't particularly care for—no doubt because it isn't energetic enough.

Living on Lake Worth as we do, fishing has always been an all-family activity. Here's Gary with his first sailfish, caught in the ocean off Palm Beach. He also wanted to make the point that it was his biggest catch to date, although he'd been hauling them in almost as heavy as himself pretty much since the time he could walk.

Cake-cutting time for John and Nancy Montgomery at their wedding Chez Nicklaus in October 1975. We've always liked to keep open house for friends, and this celebration brought in the biggest group we'd ever had, with John—who runs a third of the U.S. pro tour events—inviting golfing pals of both of us from all over the country.

Steve's no mean hand with a rod, either. Here's the first salmon he caught on a fly rod, a five-pounder, in Iceland on the way back from the British Open a few years ago.

Barbara (photo below) isn't any great fishing enthusiast, but we got her out after trout one morning in Iceland. Needless to say, all she caught was a cold.

209

Bicycles have always been big around our place—in fact, if I don't trip over one coming in, I begin to worry that everyone has gotten sick or flown the coop. Gary invited himself to join Nan and me for this nice front-yard shot, taken during a photo session for Murray Ohio, the bicycle and lawn mower company that I've been associated with for many years.

We've encouraged the children to play all sports without pushing them toward any particular one, so Jack's decision to make golf his main summer game is en-

tirely his. He's become extremely enthusiastic in recent years, and I think he could become a very good golfer if the press will only give him the opportunity to play normally like any other youngster. We've always done our best to keep the children out of the spotlight, but that's becoming more and more difficult for Jack now that he's beginning to compete in national junior events. Thank goodness, he handles these situations well and is very mature for his age. All I hope is that his love for the game remains strong enough to survive the pressures that his name subjects him to.

Page 211 shows a good follow-through, an indicator of good form throughout the earlier part of the swing. Jack has a tendency to let his right heel rise a little too quickly coming down, which sometimes throws him out and over the ball a little bit. But he's been working hard on that fault—and, as always, work pays off. His current shotmaking capability alone would put him in the mid-70s most of the time, but course-management mistakes sometimes raise his scores, especially in competition. But that, too, is improving with increased effort and growing experience.

Jack now carries a two-handicap at Lost Tree. I'm not his coach, incidentally. He listens to me out of politeness, but for the real stuff he goes to Jack Grout! Will he ever play the game professionally? That decision will be his, but he's too young and has too many other interests to start thinking about making such a big determination for a few years yet.

Say cheese! We took the opportunity of having a photographer friend on hand to get this nice family group during the World Series of Golf at Firestone in 1973. Next to me are my mother, Helen Nicklaus, and Steve. Next to Barbara are her mother and father, Helen and Stanley Bash, who that year celebrated their golden wedding anniversary. Despite all these rooters, I finished second, three shots back of Tom Weiskopf.

Typically of many fathers I know, I seemed to spend less time with Nan during her pre-teen years than with the boys, but we've been making up for that since she's formed a taste for travel. I like familiar company on the road, particularly family company, and for the past three years Nan has been a delightful companion on swings through the Continent and the Wimbledon tennis championships and then on to early practice for the British Open (Barb usually prefers to join us closer to when the real action starts). Here

we are at Carnoustie in 1976, one of us at least appropriately bonneted. We'd been in Germany for a few days, then watched Bjorn Borg and Ilie Nastase win Wimbledon semifinals. Paris is on the agenda for immediately upcoming trips, and I hope before Nan goes off and does her own thing to be able to show her all the great cities of Europe. Of course, the boys are welcome too, if they care to come along.

My mother, Helen Nicklaus, often visits with us in Florida, and we usually get together with my sister, Marilyn, and her husband, Howdy Hutchinson, and their four children when we're in Columbus. Mom's very young-looking and active for her years: still playing golf pretty regularly, *still* trying to break 119. Marilyn doesn't play golf, but she could have done so very well because she was really athletic as a youngster. The problem was she had very little interest in sports: she'd take a swing at a ball now and again, probably hit it six miles and then turn around and say, "Well, that's nice. Now what are we going to do?"

Halloween is always a big night around our neck of the woods. Here's Michael, aged three, ready for the festivities. He's supposed to be a clown, but I don't think this particular expression raised too many laughs.

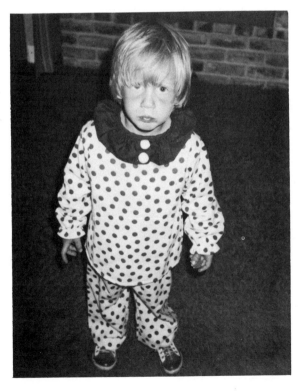

213

Gymnastics was Nan's first great sports love, and obviously it did much to develop her natural strength and agility. She gave it up as a serious endeavor a couple of years ago because she recognized there were too many other things to do, in sports and elsewhere, to be able to devote the time necessary to get really good at it. Nevertheless, as you can see here, we are occasionally treated to a few of the old moves. All the kids love to bounce around on the trampoline and on the other gymnastic gear we keep in the yard, but I don't see any Olympic champions emerging at the present time.

Much as I wanted to try it, I avoided skiing for many years because of the risk of injury. Finally, I decided that even if I didn't do it, there was no reason why the rest of the family should be deprived of the fun, and off we went to Colorado one Christmastime. All the kids fell in love with the sport immediately and have become pretty adept at it, particularly Steve, with his innate good balance and love of a new challenge. Here, he's warming up for the big stuff out in Vail.

214

I've grown to enjoy clothes, but I've never seen much point in getting dolled up around the house. Add a pair of sneakers or loafers and this is pretty much how I dress around home and office. Behind us is our pool and back porch, decorated with some of the fish various members of the family have caught.

I enjoy hunting much more for the outdoor life and the camaraderie than the actual kill, and have usually made at least one trip a year into the outback. Jack and Steve came along to New Mexico in 1976, and Jack bagged this absolutely perfect royal elk from about 175 yards, on the move, with the first rifle shot he ever fired. We enjoy wild game, and the meat made good eating for many months. The trophy, of course, occupies a position of honor in the house.

Here's an aerial view of the house—ours is the one with the tennis court next to it. Since this picture was taken, we've put in a bunker and putting green, which has encouraged me to practice the short game a little harder.

A few years ago, Eastern Airlines honored me with a sort of "This Is Your Life" evening involving our entire family and a lot of old friends from our early Columbus days. Flip Wilson was along in connection with one of his charity interests, and Gary,

who is a great fan of his, cornered him for a little golf talk. I notice Gary had gone to the interlocking grip by then!

I always spend a few days at Augusta National the week before the Masters. In 1977, for the first time, Jack took the opportunity of a midterm school holiday to come up and play the course with me and a couple of members. We played from all the way back on the tees, and I thought Jack acquitted himself well with an 80, including two putts on every green. He didn't think so, of course!

Steve, Nan and Barb at the 1977 British Open. Both the elder boys have Barbara's build—long and lean. Each of them topped my five feet eleven inches by the time he was fourteen, and I think both are going to peak probably around six-four. That's what makes Steve such a good basketball player, of course: he's very quick and strong and plays guard on our local Benjamin High School team. I think he is going to get a lot of attention from the college recruiters within a couple of years.

All of us love football, both to play and to watch. Here's Steve, number 8, just after intercepting a pass for the school team, the Benjamin Buccaneers: 1977 record 7 and 1. Steve plays safety and backup quarterback, and Jack tight end and defensive end. I'm a regular spectator, second-guesser and occasional unofficial (and, I suspect, unwanted) coach.

Here's Barbara with one of her favorite people, Edward John Stanley, the Earl of Derby, president of the British PGA. The occasion is the 1977 Ryder Cup match at Royal Lytham and St. Anne's. Lord Derby has done a great deal for professional golf over the years, and he's also great fun to be around. Barbara always makes sure we spend some time with him wherever we meet.

You can tell from the look on the faces of some of the participants that getting everyone together for this picture had intruded on much more important activities. You can also tell from the outfits what those activities were—sports. Jack must have been playing two at once, because he's wearing a football shirt with golf shoes!

Chapter 10
At Work

The Daily Routine

I probably don't spend quite the amount of time in an office that most businessmen do, but there's rarely a day when I'm at home that I'm not at a desk for at least half the working day. Frequently, that escalates to eight or more hours, particularly when business associates are in town.

Exercise has always been important to me and has become more so the older I've gotten. I almost always engage in some fairly strenuous activity each day, beginning on rising with some general conditioning exercises and following up in the late afternoon or evening with a sports activity of some sort: golf, tennis, swimming, water skiing, basketball—you name it and if it's sports I'm ready to try it. Certain of these activities, like swimming and ten-

nis, are dropped or minimized during the golf season, but the more sedentary time I spend in the office, the more adamant I become about making time for some kind of exertion, even if it's only horsing around the yard kicking or throwing a football with the kids.

Generally, I eat breakfast with the kids between seven and seven-thirty, get to the office between nine and nine-thirty, and stay there until I've finished whatever I have to do, which, if nothing else, is make a considerable number of phone calls and deal with a large amount of correspondence. Lunch is usually something light in our conference room with staff members, after which in season I'll generally either work on my golf game or play a few holes, or both.

All the kids are heavily into school or

223

local sports programs, and as both Barbara and I enjoy watching them, that's frequently our late afternoon activity. We like to eat dinner all together, which with young children means early. If nobody is coming over to visit, the rest of the evening is usually pretty relaxed, with maybe some catch-up phone calls, a little television or reading, or some activity with the children. Generally, I'm in bed by 11 P.M. and almost always asleep within about one minute of getting there.

Mark McCormack, Put Pierman and Chuck Perry

Since turning professional, I have had three exceptionally talented individuals working with me in developing various enterprises, all of whom have contributed a great deal to my business and become good personal friends as well.

My first business adviser was Mark McCormack, seen here on my left, with hometown friends Bob Hoag and Bob Barton, in 1962. (Hoagy had been a pal for years and remains one of my closest friends today. So, too, would Bob Barton be but for his tragic death in a private-plane crash on the way to the 1966 Masters.)

Mark by then had been managing athletes for a number of years, with Arnold Palmer as his star client, and I asked him to represent me when I turned professional. Prior to my making that decision, Mark had outlined some very exciting income opportunities that he felt could be developed if and when I made the change from amateur to professional. As the photo shows, we had decided on a little fun following one of our meetings. Business progress under Mark was quite good. Primarily because of my desire to manage my own business and financial affairs, Mark

and I agreed in 1970 to separate after eight years of working together, but we continue to enjoy a good personal relationship.

When this picture (page 224) was taken, Mark was, as I recall, a one- or two-handicapper. He's still a low-figure player despite his limited amount of time for golf.

Put Pierman, seen in the photo with President Ford and me (at the World Golf Hall of Fame in 1974), came on the scene as my principal business partner in 1970. Putnam is an energetic fellow, full of ideas, and he provided much excitement during the years that saw the early development of Golden Bear, Inc., and my var-

ious other business ventures—including the creation of Muirfield Village. Our relationship was a happy and fruitful one for five years, but ended amicably in 1975, when Put decided that he needed a new challenge, combined with a renewed urge on my part to totally control my own business and financial destiny.

For a while after Put's departure, I attempted to run all my affairs on a day-to-day basis, with the assistance of a number of key people. It was certainly a stimulating experience, but after a year I decided to hire an executive-search firm to help me find a top executive to take command of the operation.

Chuck Perry, shown in a recent photograph with me in our North Palm Beach offices, was named president of Golden Bear, Inc., in September 1976. Chuck (or Charles E., to be more formal) came from the communications and publishing business in New York, following several years as president of a state university in Miami. He essentially runs the business, calling on me primarily for overall policy decisions. We have an excellent relationship based upon the mutual confidence that is so important in running an effective organization.

In business, you are only as good as the people you surround yourself with, and I have been very fortunate in this regard. Mark, Put and Chuck, in addition to many others—some mentioned in this book—have helped to make my business life not only profitable but most enjoyable.

226

The Business Team

Here's a photograph of my management team taken at a meeting in early 1978 at our North Palm Beach offices. From left to right, the seated fellows are Jerry Halperin, Tom Peterson and David Sherman; standing, Chuck Perry, Ken Bowden, Bill Sansing and Jerry Pierman.

Chuck Perry, as president of Golden Bear, is responsible for the operation of all my business activities. He enjoys golf but gets to play very little these days. Bill Sansing handles our marketing and advertising activities. As a devout Texas Longhorn fan, he has chosen to make Austin his home, although he is on the road a great deal working with the various companies with which we are associated. Tom Peterson, our treasurer, is a businessman from Fort Wayne, Indiana. He's a southpaw tennis player, and a pretty good one when he gets in shape. Jerry Pierman, an occasional golfer, is our operations man and combines that task with coordinating a major portion of the golf course design division of the business. Our primary legal counsel is Dave Sherman, a partner in Dunbar, Kienzle and Murphey of Columbus, Ohio. No one's ever seen Dave with a golf club in his hand, but the word is he used to be a pretty good basketball player once upon a time. Ken Bowden, having been born in New York, raised in Melbourne and domiciled in London for much of his life, has a mixed-up accent but no difficulty in putting words on paper. A good amateur golfer, Ken handles my publishing activities. Jerry Halperin, our tax adviser, who is both a lawyer and a CPA, is a senior partner in Coopers & Lybrand and works out of Detroit. Unfortunately, this means he's also a keen supporter of University of Michigan football, but since that's his only real blemish, most of us simply try to ignore it.

These men make up my basic business team. They are also my good friends.

Our Yearly Seminar

Throughout much of the early part of my professional career, the business associations I had entered into were less productive than they might have been, for both the companies involved and me, because of a lack of close contact and communication among the various entities involved. Once I took over my own affairs, we solved that by getting everyone together each year for a three-day work-and-play seminar at which each company presents its plans and problems and gets to know everyone else on a personal basis. The integration of programs and the wealth of ideas and opportunities that have arisen have made the sessions indispensable to all concerned, and I strongly recommend a similar approach to other athletes who are involved with a complex of organizations.

Here's a typical work session during the 1973 seminar. John Allen, executive vice-president of Bostonian Shoes, is presenting our 1974 line of golfing footwear.

"State of the Union Message"

I don't know what sort of people write other sports, but I've always had a great regard for golf writers, both as a group and individually. Perhaps it's the fact that most of them play and love the game for its own sake, rather than simply for its career possibilities, that makes them such a congenial bunch of guys. Occasionally, one or two of them can be irritating with an ill-thought-out question or a quote out of context, but generally they do the job with great expertise and a lot of personal graciousness.

They have certainly been kind to me over the years, and I've always tried to return the compliment by being as available as I possibly can to any writer who wants to talk to me. As with the fans, they are an essential part of sustaining the activity that makes me a living, and if I can make their not always easy job a little less onerous, that's what I want to do. Most tour pros feel the same way. Those who don't are being extremely shortsighted, usually as the result of never having taken the trouble to establish a sound working relationship with the writers.

I'm fortunate to have a former newspaperman, Larry O'Brien, as part of my business team, and it was he who suggested some years back the activity you see here: a get-together of Florida newsmen—and any other writers who want to come—at my offices during the off-season to talk about golf and life. It has now become an annual event that is obviously helpful to the local fellows, and one that I thoroughly enjoy. Larry's title for it, "The State of the Union Message," may be a tad presumptuous, but, then, I guess you have to live with that sort of thing when a guy has spent the better part of his life looking for grabby headlines.

Modeling and Acting

The chief value most business organizations obtain from an association with me, as with all athletes, is, of course, as an advertising spokesman. Until recent years, most of this was in the print media,

which necessitated my becoming a model of sorts. There are still more than enough photo sessions every year, but lately many of the companies I'm involved with have been doing more and more television advertising. So I—and Barbara too—also had to go into the acting business. That's not really my bag, but I feel I'm getting better at it and even learning to enjoy most of it—despite what this expression, caught during a Pontiac session, might suggest to the contrary. One reason, no doubt, is that I'm trying to keep up with Barbara: despite her shyness about ever being in the limelight, she was as natural as the morning dew from the moment she first went before a camera.

Incidentally, I have always insisted upon personal approval of text and graphics or script and film in all advertising in which I'm involved.

Following are some examples of the fine work the fellows and their advertising agencies have managed to produce in recent years, despite my well-known orneriness.

MacGregor VIP–Spring, 1977

Hart Schaffner & Marx–Spring, 1977

Gleneagles–Fall, 1976

Hathaway–Spring, 1976

PUT YOURSELF IN MY SHOES

Jack Nicklaus
GOLF SHOES

Jack Nicklaus Golf Shoes (Bostonian)–Spring, 1975

NICKLAUS: Do you know me?

On the golf course, you might.

But I spend half my time as a businessman, and traveling as much as I do...

I always carry the American Express Card.

I've used it all over the world, since 1961, when I first joined the pro tour.

Hardly anyone recognized me then... but they did recognize this.

(SFX: TYPEWRITER)

ANNCR: (VO) To apply for a Card, call 800 528-8000.

NICKLAUS: The American Express Card. Don't leave home without it.

American Express TV storyboard–Spring, 1977

Jack Nicklaus puts everything he has into every drive.

GM

We do too. 1976 Pontiac Grand Prix.

There's no holding back. This year's Grand Prix shows we're shooting straight for the pin.
The dramatic new styling.
The take charge performance. A Pontiac V-8 Power steering. Power brakes. And famous Radial Tuned Suspension— all standard.
And that Grand Prix comfort to help you forget all about bogeys and bad

putts. With plush Pontiac seating. A stylish instrument panel that doglegs towards the driver for easy viewing. Plus many available luxuries... like real leather bucket seat trim, AM-FM stereo, sunroof, cruise control and more.
You may never drive like Nicklaus off the tee. But you sure can on the road. 1976 Grand Prix. At your Pontiac dealer's now.

PONTIAC
The Mark of Great Cars

Pontiac–Spring, 1976

Yards of difference

Smooth, controlled power. It makes the difference in Jack Nicklaus' outstanding golf swing, also makes the difference in Murray's outstanding lawn equipment...yards of difference.

Now, Murray's new Medalist line of lawn tractors, riders and walking mowers offers outstanding features to fit every task and every budget. See the Jack Nicklaus tag and the new Murray Medalists at your dealer, or write us for the dealer nearest you.

The Medalists from MURRAY
THE MURRAY OHIO MFG. CO., BRENTWOOD, TENN. 37027

Murray Ohio–Spring, 1978

Magic Chef–Fall, 1977

Slazenger™ (Australia)–Fall, 1977

Vigoro–Spring, 1978

Apparel group (Japan)–Fall, 1977

Lotus (U.K.)–Year round, 1976

Terex–Fall, 1977

Chapter 11
At Leisure

Fishing

I've loved fishing, almost all kinds, ever since my golf coach, Bob Kepler, introduced me to fly casting back in my early days at Ohio State. Nothing made Kep happier than to run a bunch of us out to the Zanesfield Rod and Gun Club, an hour west of Columbus, and teach us that intricate art. I always had the feeling he loved being on the water much more than on the golf course, fine golf coach that he was. Here's Jackie out at Zanesfield with me in the fall of 1966, looking for rainbow trout. He likes to fish as much as I do and for the same reason: by eating what's eatable and releasing what isn't or what you don't need, you can get your relaxation and your challenge without needlessly destroying anything.

I certainly have been fortunate through my golfing travels to have been able to try for a great variety of fish. Early in my Florida days, as these three pictures show, I got pretty wrapped up in deep-sea fishing, and I still enjoy it, particularly for sailfish. These days, we like to mix it up more, with maybe a trip or two for permit or bonefish and another at a different time of year

for salmon or trout. Recently, I've tacked a spell of fishing onto many of my trips to play abroad, which is an excellent way to rest the mind from golf before or after an important tournament. Here's a snap from one of those R and R sessions, in Iceland.

Boats

Enjoying ocean fishing so much, I got pretty hooked on boats when we first moved to Florida. The first thing I found out about them is that they are expensive, and the second thing I found out about them—as this picture shows—is that they are not all glamour and glory. We've had a variety over the years from large to small. Nowadays, we've settled for a couple of small ones that the kids can handle easily, chartering something bigger for anything more than lake or offshore fishing.

Tennis

I love tennis and at one time played a lot of it all through the year, both for the fun and because it is so good for my legs. Recently, the rotary swinging actions involved have tended to aggravate a slight back problem caused by golf, resulting in muscle spasms, so I've quit the game during the golf season. Occasionally, I've broken that rule, as in the first picture here, following a win in the Tournament of Champions in 1973. It was a chilly evening, and I think it was that as much as anything that tempted me onto the La Costa courts.

How good am I? Well, note the marvelous form in the other picture: the fine balance, well-positioned head, nice weight distribution, sighting finger fully extended, complete follow-through. Actually, it looks more like the finish of a golf swing than a tennis stroke!

Seriously, I have a strong first serve, a reasonable twist second serve, a fairly reliable forehand, and not too much of a backhand.

239

Basketball

As I mentioned earlier, basketball was my top sport after golf in high school, and I took it up again about four years ago, playing a couple of nights a week in winter leagues whenever I'm at home. The picture here was snapped during a student-faculty game early in 1976 before the school the elder children attend had a gymnasium. I'm not actually on the faculty, but I spend so much time working on sports with some of its members that they usually invite me along as a sort of ex officio team member.

We built an excellent gymnasium a couple of years ago, plus a new football field. The school is excellent academically, and because I feel so strongly about the role of sports in children's development, I wanted to lend a hand in ensuring that its athletic programs were up to the same standards. Here are Barbara, Nan and I at one of the school's games there, talking with coach Mickey Neal (left, with tie), who is also a close friend.

Skiing

Here's a sport I could really become nutty about. It's challenging, it's great exercise, it's exhilarating, and it's a marvelous family activity. I recognize that it is also dangerous, and I get a lot of flak about that from friends and colleagues—but so, if you want to look at it that way, is getting out of bed in the morning. You have to live life.

I started skiing during the 1975 Christmas holidays and have been on the slopes every Christmastime since. We get in a couple of other short trips, usually on the way back from the Crosby. I don't take any unnecessary chances. I have never skied an inch of mountainside without an instructor along. What tickles me is how well the kids have taken to it: all of them fell in love with it the moment they tried it.

Hunting

I hunt occasionally, mainly for fowl and for the pleasure of the backcountry and the challenges involved. We also make a point of shooting only what we can eat and eating everything we shoot. Here's Jackie's first hunting experience, back around Christmastime of 1966. The fellow on the left, Bill Kaeneman, a friend from Illinois, took us out for geese, the first and only time I've hunted such quarry.

I've seldom practiced shooting, but I'm a decent shot, as this picture would seem to indicate. We were hunting elk in New Mexico in 1973 when we came across some turkey. Most hunters in those parts usually take a shotgun along against such a possibility, but not having one, I took a crack with a rifle and caught him clean on the dead run. We had him for Thanksgiving dinner.

Baseball

I'll play a little backyard baseball once in a while, but I no longer have those major league dreams of junior-high days. This picture was taken during a spell in the early seventies when I was helping to coach the local Little League team that Jack played on. Hitting fungo flies, by the looks of it. I think I had more fun than the kids!

Scuba Diving

I've done a lot of snorkeling over the years off the coasts of Florida and the Bahamas, but this was the first time I ever tried scuba diving. We were fishing off the Great Barrier Reef, north of Australia, and the mate on our boat happened to be an instructor. You need a little while to get the hang of it, but it's great fun when you do.

Bicycling

One definite change in the golf tour during my years out there has been the ever-increasing athleticism of the players. Most of the better golfers have always taken pretty good care of themselves, but there weren't too many truly athletically fit fellows on the tour when I joined it in 1962. Now a high proportion are just that, especially among the younger players. As I said in *Golf My Way*, I'm certain that continually playing other sports—and especially highly exertive sports like tennis and basketball—has had a tremendous influence on my game. I might still be out there without having done all that physical activity, but I'm certain I wouldn't be the factor that I still believe I am.

The key part of the body for every golfer, of course, is the legs, because they are the first to go with age. I don't do a whole lot of bicycling, but I would if, like many golfers, I had no other convenient way to keep my legs in shape, because it's a perfect exercise for them.

Chapter 12
Technique

Controlled Power

Here's a picture from my early twenties, when I was at the peak of my strength. Finesse was entering into the game more and more at this point, but I could still rely on raw power whenever I needed it. I'm hitting the ball extremely hard in this picture, but the form indicates I was doing so with a well-controlled swing. I particularly like the firmness and "one-pieceness" of the left side and the way I am swinging my arms and shoulders "under" my head. No coming over the ball here. Note how the club shaft and left arm have returned to a straight line at impact. You mustn't release too early with the wrists; but on the other hand, you have to get the clubhead into the ball before your hands have passed it if you are going to hit it solidly in the back.

Cocking the Wrists

There are different schools of thought as to when the wrists should hinge or cock. I've always belonged to the one that believes they should only do so in response to the swinging momentum of the club-head as it rises to a point where it begins to exert a pull on the hands and arms. The reason is that an earlier, more deliberate cocking might inhibit the one-piece take-away of the club from the ball that is essential to establish the full turn and maximum arm extension that I regard as imperative to a powerful game. In short, if I

hinged my wrists earlier, it might lead to an incomplete backswing through a too quick lifting of the club. Here's the point in the swing where the momentum of the rising club begins the gradual cocking of my wrists. With the longer clubs, as I start down this hinging is slightly increased by the pull of my lower body toward the target.

The "Flying Right Elbow"

Here are two angles on what people call my "flying right elbow." It's certainly high, but that goes with my upright swing plane and determination to achieve the maximum possible upper-body coiling and arm extension. From here, as the other two pictures show, the elbow is pulled straight down toward my right hip by my lower-body action. If it weren't, if I started down with my hands and shoulders, like most amateurs, the club would be thrown forward—in which case I'd probably still be selling insurance for a living.

Hand-Wrist-Forearm Alignment

I play my best when the back of my left hand, wrist and forearm form a straight line at the top, as seen here. I regard this position as "square," in the sense that it requires no manipulation of the club by the hands and arms, either going up or coming down, in order to deliver it squarely to the ball. If my wrists were cupped or concave at this point, I'd have to manipulate the club or my body in some way in order not to make contact with the face open. If they were arched or convex, I'd need another kind of manipulation in order not to arrive at the ball with a closed clubface. Occasionally, a very good player can make these kinds of compensations when he's feeling particularly well-coordinated and there's little pressure on him, but they are rarely manageable under win-or-lose tournament pressures.

The Shaft at the Top

Here's a piece of "geometry" I strive for on all full shots: the club shaft at the top paralleling the intended flight line. If the club crosses the line—points right of target—I'll tend to hook or push the ball by coming at it too much from the inside. If the club were to be laid off—pointed left of target—I'd tend to deliver it from outside the target line, pulling or slicing the shot.

You've Got to Go Back Before You Come Down

Most golfers lack power because they simply don't get enough of themselves *back* far enough before starting down to the ball. These three shots from various periods of my career show what I'm talking about. Obviously, the mechanics of the motion are important, but if you want distance you must have clubhead speed, and if you want clubhead speed you must have leverage, and if you want leverage you must coil—you must *wind up*. Static feet, legs and hips are a common problem among handicappers: many players are so control-conscious that they never let their lower bodies get fully into the act, which forces them to flail weakly at the ball with just their hands and arms. Note here how far the torsion in my upper body has turned my hips and pulled the left knee back past the ball, and note also the heel lift. There's no way I could get the shoulder turn and arm extension that I do without these lower-body actions. The important thing is to let them occur in *response* to the upper-body coiling, not as generators of it, otherwise the turn will lack torque and thus the reactive leverage that creates clubhead speed.

Pull the Club Down, Don't "Throw" It

For effective golf, the club must be *pulled*, not thrown, from the top of the backswing until its centrifugal force becomes so great that the hands and wrists are forced to release in order to sustain its momentum through the ball. All good players generate that pulling motion by uncoiling from the top of the backswing from the feet upward. Almost all poor players destroy it by throwing from the top part of the body before the lower body can go to work. I think these three pictures nicely capture the sense of pulling, with the hands, arms and club obviously trailing the targetward leg and hip action.

Golf's Absolute Fundamental

I've always regarded a steady head as the absolute fundamental of golf, the number-one tenet for every player irrespective of his inherent capabilities or his natural or chosen swing style. The reason is simple: if you move your head, you alter the arc and plane the clubhead describes, which makes it extremely difficult to meet the ball solidly without a counterbalancing movement. Golf's difficult enough without that. Here are a couple of examples of keeping the head steady. Basically, I set it in position behind the ball at address, cock my chin to the right just before I start the club back to make maximum room for the fullest possible shoulder turn, then keep it there until the momentum of the follow-through naturally pulls it around so that my eyes can track the flight of the ball.

Clubhead "Geometry"

Many handicappers would play better if they had a clearer conception of the proper path of the clubhead and the correct action of the clubface through and beyond the ball. Going back, the clubface opens (its toe moves farther away from the ball than its heel) as the club swings inside the target line in response to the turning of the shoulders. Going through—as seen here—the clubface closes as it again swings inside the target line in response to the unwinding of the body. The trick of golf is simply to make the moment when the clubface is square to the target and traveling exactly along the target line coincide with impact. That isn't easy; but on the other hand, you won't play any better by trying to "hold" or force the clubhead to stay square and the clubhead path to follow the target line well beyond impact. All you'll do is inhibit the free-swinging motion that produces distance.

251

The Hands Must Cross at Some Point

If the club is to swing inside the target line and the clubface to close naturally after impact, the left hand must turn over and the right hand cross over it at some point beyond impact. Here's a sequence of that action. The art lies in not allowing the left hand and wrist to break down—to buckle or cup—before impact, which requires a full clearance of the hips in order to make room for the hands and arms to swing freely past the body. Understand, too, that the faster the hands turn over through the impact area, the more hook spin will be imparted to the ball; and the slower or less they cross, the more likely the chance of slicing or pushing the ball by hitting it with the clubface open.

252

Plane Comparisons Tell a Lot

Photography, both still and movie, can be very helpful in identifying and correcting swing flaws that you can't "feel" and that are difficult for even a trained observer to spot with the naked eye. For example, the plane of the swing on the follow-through tells quite a lot about the initial downswing action. Ideally, the plane coming through should be pretty much the same as the plane going back. If it's flatter, chances are there was too much upper-body or hand and arm movement starting the downswing, causing the club to be thrown forward before the legs got fully to work. If it's steeper, there's probably a need for earlier or stronger hip clearance to make more room for the hands and arms to swing past the body and thus obviate a "blocking" action through the ball. Looks in both these pictures as though my downswing-initiating moves were good, in that the follow-through planes are very close to those of my backswing.

Maximize Your Best Physical Assets

Smart golfers maximize their greatest physical assets in developing and building a swing. For example, because he had such large and powerful hands, Tommy Armour built his game around hand and wrist action, whereas Arnold Palmer, with his unusually strong upper body, has been essentially a shoulder swinger. The strongest part of my body is my legs, and I've always tried to use them to maximum effect in the swing. Here's the through-swing leg action that is the basis of my long game and the source of my power. Note that it varies by degree depending on the type of shot I'm playing: in the first picture, I'm hitting a normally flighted nine-iron; in the second, I'm trying to drive the ball low with a long-iron. Essentially, the higher you want to hit the ball, the less leg and the more hand and wrist action you use; and the lower you want to fly it, the more you drive with your legs and the longer you delay the wrist and hand release.

254

How My Game Has Changed

As this book was being completed, I had just concluded my twenty-fifth straight year of tournament golf and was coming up on my thirty-eighth birthday. How did my game stand at that time, and what did I see for it in the future?

As an amateur, I was essentially a one-dimensional golfer: a left-to-right player. I was also mostly a one-style golfer: hit it hard, find it, and hit it hard again. Strength was, of course, a big factor in both those characteristics. I was so strong that I almost *had* to play from left to right to be able to control the ball, and I could certainly well afford to give up whatever distance I lost by fading rather than drawing shots in return for that greater control. Also, the amount of raw strength I had at my disposal tended to make me somewhat cavalier about the sorts of problems that less powerful players usually rely upon finesse to overcome. Frequently, I could simply whale the ball *over* obstacles that others would prefer to finesse their way around with artfully flighted shots. So far as rough was concerned, with all that strength and an upright swing plane, and being generally a good way out from the tee, I encountered very little from which I couldn't bulldoze the ball either onto the green or very close to it. The "explosive" method, I guess you could call it. Distance first and worry about everything else after that. It was an effective way to play at the time, but hardly the most graceful approach to the game.

For several years, I played basically the same way as a professional, but eventually I realized the need for some improvements and refinements and gradually began to make them. A variety of factors contributed to these changes, but the primary one was my own personal golfing ambition. I wanted to be the best, and I increasingly recognized from studies of the great players—not to mention my day-to-day observations of them as tour adversaries—that the absolute basic requirement in achieving such a goal was the ability to play any given shot at any given time, including those moments involving extreme tension and stress. Another factor was pride. Simply to satisfy myself, I wanted to make myself as good a golfer technically as it was possible for me to become.

The improvement process has been going on now for some twelve years or more, and I expect it to continue for as long as I remain competitive at the game. Basically, I've learned as I've gone along, rarely more than one thing at a time, always working within the framework of the fundamentals imparted to me as a teenager by Jack Grout and always using essentially the same golf swing. My initial improvements were primarily in the long game: learning first to control the height of shots and then to draw the ball as easily and reliably as I have always been able to fade it. Bunker techniques have been remodeled or revised on a number of occasions, as have basic approaches to pitching and chipping. Being so largely a matter of feel and inspiration, putting has always undergone almost daily fine tuning, and sometimes drastic surgery, from one green to the next—but, again, always within the framework of what I believe to be the sound stroking mechanics I learned as a youngster.

And the sum of this long effort? Well, the first thing I have learned is that you never stop learning about golf, which is probably the single greatest source of the game's enormous appeal to so many disparate people around the world. Beyond that, although I am not as powerful a golfer as I was in my twenties, it seems to me that I more than make up for whatever I have lost in distance and bulldozing capacity with greatly improved shotmaking versatility. I wouldn't say there aren't golf shots I can't hit to order these days, but I *would* say they are fairly few in number. That wasn't true of my amateur days or my first few years on tour.

The greatest improvement, however, hasn't been in shotmaking but in the area of the game that I have always believed finally sorts out the wheat from the chaff—and the one, incidentally, most neglected by most amateurs of more than a six-handicap. This is the art, craft or science of scoring. Hitting the ball is really only half the game of golf. Once you become reasonably adept at that, how well you play—how often you win or lose—depends almost entirely on how effectively you learn to manage the game's two ultimate adversaries: the course and yourself. Managing the course takes patience, the discipline to train yourself to be habitually observant and analytic, and the kind of knowledge that can be gained only by study and experience. Managing yourself requires intelligence and emotional control. Both, like learning to hit the shots, require perseverance. In theory, maturity builds all these resources, and in my case I believe it has done so now, to the point where I can consider these aspects of my game to be my strongest competitive weapons.

So, in short, I think I'm a better golfer today than I have ever been.

And the future? God willing, I intend to get better yet.